PRAISE FOR

THE MONSTER UNDER THE BED

"My counsel to any CEO—or to any executive who wants to be one—is simple: Ignore this book at your peril! Davis and Botkin rightly define customers as learners, businesses as educators, and knowledge as the key to success in the new world order in commerce."

—Melvin R. Goodes,
Chairman and CEO, Warner-Lambert Company

"*The Monster Under the Bed* is future visioning at its best. This book will challenge cherished assumptions, provoke debate, and stimulate thinking—just what is needed to help us prepare for a future where only one thing is certain, uncertainty itself."
—Peter M. Senge, M.I.T., author of *The Fifth Discipline*

"Stan Davis and Jim Botkin persuasively argue that responsibility for education is passing from government to business. *The Monster* richly deserves to be widely read and will change the context of the debate about education in the United States."
—John Naisbitt, author of *Global Paradox* and *Megatrends*

"Learning is at the center of the knowledgescape—not just individual and organizational learning, but also products, products that learn. *The Monster Under the Bed* is a must for understanding how learning technologies are transforming our work and our play, our businesses and our schools, our entire lives."
—John Seely Brown, Xerox, Chief Scientist

ALSO BY STAN DAVIS

2020 Vision
Future Perfect

ALSO BY JIM BOTKIN

No Limits to Learning
Global Stakes

THE
MONSTER
UNDER THE BED

HOW BUSINESS IS MASTERING
THE OPPORTUNITY OF
KNOWLEDGE FOR PROFIT

STAN DAVIS AND JIM BOTKIN

SIMON & SCHUSTER

NEW YORK   LONDON   TORONTO   SYDNEY   TOKYO   SINGAPORE

SIMON & SCHUSTER
Rockefeller Center
1230 Avenue of the Americas
New York, New York 10020

Copyright © 1994 by Stanley M. Davis and James W. Botkin

Designed by Irving Perkins Associates
Manufactured in the United States of America

1   3   5   7   9   10   8   6   4   2

Library of Congress Cataloging-in-Publication Data
Davis, Stanley M.
    The monster under the bed : how business is mastering the
opportunity of knowledge for profit / Stan Davis and Jim Botkin.
        p.   cm.
    Includes bibliographical references.
    1. Business education.   2. Industry and education.   3. Employees—
Training of.   4. Information technology.   5. Continuing education.
6. Competition.   I. Botkin, James W.   II. Title.
HF1106.D32   1994
331.25'92—dc20   94—12549
                                                               CIP

ISBN: 0-671-87107-2

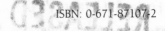

*For
Rick and Len Davis
and
Alexi and Chris Botkin*

CONTENTS

Chapter 3: THE CHATTER, THE STRING, AND THE CAN 61

Chapter 4: L'EARNING POWER 84

CHAPTER 5: THE *LAST* THING YOU WANT IS A LEARNING ORGANIZATION 109

CHAPTER 6: THE SIX R'S 132

CHAPTER 7: FOR BETTER AND FOR WORSE 157

*always the beautiful answer
who asks a more beautiful question.*

——E. E. CUMMINGS

*. . . to lay bare the questions
which have been hidden by the answers.*

—JAMES BALDWIN

THE SEVEN WAYS

The field cannot well be seen from within the field.

—RALPH WALDO EMERSON

Megan was five years old and worried about a monster that lived under her bed. She told a story about how the monster scared her, how she wanted it to go away, and how she solved the problem—now the monster lives under her brother's bed. She also drew pictures to accompany the story. They look like the kind displayed by parents on refrigerator doors, only Megan drew these pictures on her computer and used the computer to record her telling of the tale. It was all done with a software package geared to kids her age.

Megan didn't stop there. She wanted to share her story, so she sent it by phone to an electronic bulletin board club, where other kids her age could watch and hear it. This, in turn, was picked up by Nautilus, a CD-ROM multimedia magazine, and that was how we happened upon it on one of our computers.

When we clicked on Megan's story we were amazed. It lasted less than a minute, and we watched it five times. Here was a five-year-old child who had accomplished all the major tasks of moviemaking. She was the star, wrote the screenplay, created the visuals, did the editing,

*was producer and director, and even did her own distribution. Her
learning was integrated into the realities of her life. And to her it was
all play.*

THE MONSTER UNDER MEGAN'S BED

Children have been seeing monsters under their beds and telling
their families and friends about them for centuries. This is nothing new. What *is* new is the way Megan told her story—and how
she learned to do it.

Just a generation ago, if Megan's mother had wanted to tell a
similar tale, she would have written words and drawn pictures
with paint or crayon on a piece of paper. And she would have
learned to write and draw in school, under the watchful guidance
of a teacher. Megan did not yet know how to write, but she knew
how to use a computer. She learned how to use it at home, with
the help of the computer itself.

Similar learning is going on now for people of all ages, at home
and in the workplace. The monster under Megan's bed may have
been imaginary, but the electronic technology she used to describe it is undeniably real and has begun to assume its own
monstrous proportions.

Countless companies and business alliances are providing electronic products and services to millions of people like Megan and
her family, bringing them entertainment and education at home
and on the job. These companies are in the knowledge business—
knowledge for profit—and they are revolutionizing the way we
learn at the same time as they are creating a powerful new opportunity for growth in business.

For many people, the real monsters under the bed are the old
corporate dinosaurs that won't change. For others, it's the specter
of technology run amok. Behind it all looms a gargantuan
government-run education system incapable of handling a doubling of knowledge about every seven years. The knowledge revolution will power the new global economy, reshape many of our

institutions—particularly education—and touch every aspect of our lives. Business sees the opportunity, and it is driving ahead full speed to realize this vision to adapt to, and profit from, the realities of the new information economy.

We may speak glibly of the "knowledge revolution," but what does it mean if knowledge is becoming the resource adding the most value to business and the economy? What can business do to profit from the knowledge revolution? How can you, as a consumer, profit from knowledge products and services rather than be intimidated by them?

The knowledge business is transforming the way we learn. But will the new learning business deliver information, knowledge, and education in such different ways and vast amounts that it parallels, rivals, and in some instances even displaces schools as the major deliverer of learning? Are we ending schooling as we have known it? In consequence, will we run our economy differently? Will we raise and educate our children differently? Finally, how will the knowledge revolution alter the very fabric of our society?

The answers to these questions are already discernible in the business world, in education, and in society as a whole. In broad outline business is mastering the opportunity presented by the knowledge revolution in seven significant ways.

THE SEVEN WAYS

First, business is coming to bear the major responsibility for the kind of education that is necessary for any country to remain competitive in the new economy.

Business, more than government, is instituting the changes in education that are required for the emerging knowledge-based economy. School systems, public or private, are lagging behind the transformation in learning that is evolving outside of schools, in the private sector at both work and play, for people of all ages. Computer skills, for example, are critical to national competitiveness today, yet only a small portion of the sixty million personal computer owners learned to use their PCs in school. The vast majority, like Megan, learned either as consumers at home or as employees at work. Over the next few decades the private sector will eclipse the public sector and become the major institution responsible for learning.

Second, the marketplace for learning is being redefined dramatically from K–12 to K–80, or lifelong learning, whose major segments are customers, employees, and students, in that order.

A new meaning of education and learning is bursting on the scene in America. Education for earlier economies was front-ended. When America was an agrarian economy, education for young people between seven and fourteen was sufficient to last the forty years of a working life. In the industrial economy, the age range of students expanded to between five and twenty-two. In the information economy, the rapid pace of technological change means that education must be updated throughout our working lives. People have to increase their learning power to sustain their earning power. Lifelong learning is the norm that is augmenting and in some cases displacing school-age education.

Employees, for example, are a major new learning segment. Because knowledge is doubling nearly every seven years, in technical fields specifically, half of what students learn in their first year of college is obsolete by the time they graduate. In the labor force the need to keep pace with technological change is felt even more acutely. For companies to remain competitive and workers to be employable, they must continue to learn. This shadow education market is underestimated. Employee learning is a lot more than just training and development (T&D). Motorola spends $120 million on employee education, Arthur Andersen spends 6.5 percent of revenues, and Saturn requires one hundred hours per year of formal learning for each management and union employee.

Students and schools will be the last segment to experience the changes that are imminent. Student education will remain largely in the public sector, and school leaders will continue to try to reform the old system rather than embrace the new forms that will ultimately prevail.

Third, any business can become a knowledge business by putting data and information to productive use, creating knowledge-based products and services that make its customers smarter.

Consumers will be the newest and largest learning segment in the twenty-first-century marketplace. As information technologies become so much friendlier and smarter, and as they become intrinsic to more and more products and services, learning becomes a by-product (and by-service) of the customers' world. Never before in history have customers considered themselves learners, nor to such a great degree have businesses considered themselves educators.

The progression began with businesses that provided the technical function of data processing and then advanced to the broader activity of information management. It is now moving into its next phase: information technology whose chief and most valuable task is to provide knowledge. When a portable wireless fax machine knows how to find a recipient any time, any place, that's a knowledge-based technology. In the years ahead more and more companies will add knowledge-based features to their products and services, increasing their economic value to both the company and the customer.

Fourth, a new generation of smart and humanized technologies will revolutionize learning by employees and customers in business before it affects students and teachers in schools.

Today's developments in technology are no less profound than when Gutenberg's printing press and Bible broke the church's monopoly on what was taught and by whom. Our technologies are not making teachers and schools obsolete, but they are redefining their roles, and with the increasing use of these technologies to reach learners directly, schools are often bypassed entirely.

We see this, for example, in interactive multimedia and in the emerging "edutainment" industry. Magazines, books, TV programs, movies, databases, and software all provide information and knowledge that are directly available to customers. The methods of delivery may be computers, phones, TVs, recorders, and faxes, and all are currently in use by consumers and businesses, and to a lesser degree by schools and students.

Electronic technology has evolved in stages, centered on providing first data, then information, and now knowledge. Moreover, these three stages parallel the three major learning markets—students, employees, and consumers. Student education, in a holdover from the rote learning of the industrial period, focuses more on the mastery of data than do employee and customer learning. Employee education, experiencing an explosive period of growth that parallels the post–data information period of the last twenty years, concentrates on information. Customer learning and education, on the other hand, is just now beginning its growth phase, and as the humanization of information technology speeds up, it will emphasize knowledge.

Fifth, business-driven learning will be organized according to the values of today's information age: service, productivity, customization, networking, and the need to be fast, flexible, and global.

How will the information age affect ways businesses organize? Today most of the economy is centered on service activities, but only some businesses are organized to deliver services. Thus it would be logical to assume that all businesses will evolve organizations that more directly support the services they provide. Frontline people in service businesses, for example, have direct customer contact and use electronic technology daily. Yet the outmoded organizations of many of these businesses promote people up and away from the customer and away from technology. Organizing around service will mean finding ways to promote people toward, not away from, customers and technology.

It will also mean that customers, as well as suppliers and distributors, will be able electronically to enter directly into the core of an organization. Customers can self-track their packages, for example, on Federal Express's knowledge-based system, which is a key component in providing quality service and customer satisfaction.

The same kind of logic can be applied to the emphases on productivity, networking, time-based competition, and other values of the information economy. American business has learned to become more productive, which has resulted in its current strength relative to much of business in Europe and Japan. This increased productivity has resulted, first and foremost, from redesigning the way companies were organized. The organization model of the industrial economy emphasized a division of labor and was chronically hampered by problems of lateral coordination among different units. Today's networking technologies, however, have tied together diverse groups that would otherwise be separated by geography and reporting structures. Knowledge-based businesses are rewriting the rule books for how we organize.

Sixth, schools will embrace businesslike practices to improve their own performance. The three R's will be complemented by the new six R's: risks, results, rewards, relationships, research, and rivalry.

Education in public sector schools, like that provided by church and family, will not disappear in the information economy. Such institutions serve an important socializing role in addition to their purely educational functions. They will continue to survive in some places, but in smaller pockets and for specific age groups. Public school systems do not have the right format for providing the kind of lifelong education that will best serve the future needs of our economy and society. Where they will thrive, in the language of business, is where they become specialized niche players.

"The best thing about the future," said Abe Lincoln, "is that it only comes one day at a time." Thus, slowly, schools will take advantage of new information technology, emphasize many businesslike values in their teaching, and adopt many businesslike practices in their organization. Colleges routinely say good-bye to their best customers at graduation, for example, rather than turn them into lifelong learner/customers. Business knows that retaining an old customer is far better than finding a new one.

Other applicable business practices that will find their way into public education include the ability to manage *r*isks, focus on *r*esults, and use *r*ewards as incentives. Schools will also deepen their *r*elationships with the institutions that employ their graduates, engage in *r*esearch for their future at a level comparable to that done in the business world, and, like business, view competition or *r*ivalry as a healthy tonic. Eventually these new six R's of education will far better serve the needs of students and the needs of business when these students become employees.

Seventh, the revolution in the way we learn will worsen the already grave division between social classes, requiring us to redress human and social inequities.

Unfettered capitalism bred significant inequalities in income distribution and social justice and created the socialist and communist backlash. Although those alternatives finally failed, we are once again confronted with the danger of a growing chasm between haves and have-nots in our society, and the knowledge revolution runs the risk of increasing this gap even more than it presents the likelihood of closing it. It is the dark side of what is otherwise a thrilling awakening, a potential trend we ignore at our peril.

Will business be any better at correcting these ills than either the church or government before it? Our system of learning is a reflection of our social, political, and economic needs. When these needs shift direction, changes in how and what we learn are sure to follow. We are once again at just such a major shift.

The breakup of the Soviet Union eliminated a major threat to our democracy, although as an unintended consequence, it also diminished our political incentive to reinvigorate education. Economically, however, the rise of Japan and Germany is a wake-up call to America. Also, China's economy is suddenly growing five times as fast as ours and, despite low per capita wealth, is one of the largest in the world, already third behind the United States and Japan. Today the changes in how we learn are being driven more by economics than by politics.

Business is enmeshed in a historical process from which it cannot escape. Quite the reverse. It stands to benefit from a period of new growth. The revolution in learning that is already under way has the power to create a booming economy and to transform even the oldest businesses and school systems into newly dynamic and productive institutions. The learning revolution will have many consequences, some good, some bad, others unpredictable. Its life cycle will last many decades, some heady and others contentious. It will leave no one unaffected. That is why we must understand clearly what is happening to learning and knowledge.

KNOWLEDGE FOR PROFIT

There are many ways to profit from knowledge. Some are very lofty and some rather mundane. Some come from experience and some necessitate study. Some require an understanding of how to deal with people and some of how to deal with things. However it is acquired, however it is applied, knowledge is of central importance to a thriving economy.

That is why a revolution in the way we learn is unfolding in the United States and why there has come to be an increasing alliance between business and learning. Each country, however, has its own culture, history of education, and experience with business. Even in those countries where business is underdeveloped or oppressive, many people are searching to find an alternative to a government monopoly on learning. Although the American experience is, in many ways, unique, the examples and alternatives that are emerging in this country may serve as useful models for many other countries and cultures.

Today knowledge is often a business's most valuable commodity, and knowledge workers are often its most valuable resource. Knowledge is an increasing portion of the value of an offering in the marketplace and the basis for competitive advantage. Education and learning are becoming intrinsic and highly valued in the processes, products, services, and organization of business. Similarly, business is evolving new ways that will revolutionize learning and ultimately free education from the failed hegemony of public schools and the dominance of government.

Many business leaders will be unprepared for this revolution. Many educators and parents will feel threatened by what they see as an intrusion of private enterprise into a public responsibility. At the same time, many are already frustrated by the slow pace of reform in schools and feel instinctively that our system is falling behind. More and more time seems to be spent preparing for jobs and careers that will no longer exist on graduation day, and many students welcome more involvement with business. Business itself is a reluctant heir to its new responsibilities as educator. But both business and education are important to each other and to society.

This book is an examination of current and future trends in the knowledge revolution. The way Megan told the story of the monster under her bed is only the tip of the iceberg. She will grow up in a world in which the smart products and services made possible by information technology will play a major role. They will change the way she is educated, the way she works, and the way she leads her everyday life. These changes are already under way. In writing about them, we intend primarily to alert business to new opportunities for growth, as well as to the need for educating both employees and customers to maintain that growth. Additionally, we intend to alert educators to new and broader contexts, so that the future can come in as a friend, not a foe.

We see exciting and challenging times ahead for business and education within the context of the burgeoning growth of knowledge technology. Everyone will be profoundly affected by it, and it is our hope that this book will be a personal awakening to new possibilities that will help all of us meet and master the challenges ahead.

CHAPTER 1

THE RELUCTANT HEIR

Most of the learning in use is of no great use.

—BENJAMIN FRANKLIN

FROM CHURCH TO STATE TO BUSINESS

Through successive periods of history, different institutions have borne the major responsibility for education. Changes in education take a very long time to evolve. They are a consequence of greater transformations, often social, political, economic, or religious, and therefore are always a few steps behind the demands of the society they are designed to serve. But today schools are more than a few steps behind, and many feel they are on the wrong path altogether.

Ben Franklin, James Madison, and Patrick Henry were all taught at home rather than in school. In colonial America, the kitchen was the schoolhouse, mother was the teacher, and church was the overseer. As the agrarian economy expanded, children were educated in one-room schoolhouses. With the move from an agrarian to an industrial economy, the small rural schoolhouse was supplanted by the big brick urban schoolhouse. Four decades ago, in the early 1950s, we began the move to another economy, but we have yet to develop a new educational paradigm, let alone create the "schoolhouse" of the future, which may be neither school nor house.

The coming shift from civil to commercial leadership in education has been evolving for decades, and it will take several decades more before it is complete. The first great educational shift, from church to state dominance, followed a similar progression. How and why it happened helps explain the current and coming change.

THE FIRST TIME 'ROUND

Education in America was dominated by church and family from the earliest European settlements until the end of the colonial period in the 1780s.[1] Family, church, school, and civic authority were intermingled during this early period, although the family had the greatest influence. *The Family Instructor,* by Daniel Defoe (1715), was as popular in pre–Revolutionary America as Dr. Spock was in the post–World War II United States. Most family education, however, was on religious matters. The guiding books were John Foxe's *The Book of Martyrs* (1563) and Lewis Bayly's *The Practice of Piety* (1612). Christianity, like Judaism from which it emanated, has always been an educational system, with Christ as the divine teacher. Harvard's stated purpose, for example, was instruction to "know God and Jesus Christ."

Church control of education was exercised by the Puritans in New England, the Dutch Reformed Church and Quakers in the mid-Atlantic region, and powerful Protestant and Catholic plantation families in the South, especially Virginia. There were also many other churches, sects, and religions, and competition among them led to the expansion of education.

The debate about whether church or state should be responsible for education went on for over a hundred years before the Revolutionary War. It started in 1655, when a Harvard president was forced to resign over the issue of infant baptism. Another challenge to the church was repeated almost a century later when the *Independent Whig,* distributed from Boston to Savannah, declared: "The ancients were instructed by philosophers, and the moderns by priests. The first thought it their duty to make the students as useful as possible to their country; the latter as subservient to their order." Twelve decades later, with the Revolutionary War and the Constitution, which clearly delineated a separation between church and state, the responsibility for public education was assumed primarily by the state.

The changing of the guard from church to state was propelled chiefly by political rather than economic motives. In New England it took five decades after the Revolutionary War until the Puritans and the Congregational Church relinquished their domination of schools. It occurred first in 1827, when, by taxation, Massachusetts made the support of public schools compulsory. Public support of schools in the South did not occur until after the Civil War, nearly nine decades after ratification of the United States Constitution in 1789 and the Ordinance of 1787, which established "education as necessary to good government."

Only after independence from England did education begin to move from parent and pastor to schoolmaster and governmental authorities. The motivating factor was the need to build a free and independent government. The chief educators of the time, Benjamin Franklin and Thomas Jefferson, were first and foremost political figures. As early as 1749, Franklin, in his *Proposals Relating to the Education of Youth in Pennsylvania,* announced a plan to establish a grammar school in Philadelphia that would use English, the vernacular of trade and daily life, rather than Latin, the language of the church.

Fifty years later, in 1779, Jefferson introduced a "Bill for the More General Diffusion of Knowledge" in the Virginia Legislature, mandating that all children be educated at public expense, which made education a political rather than a religious function. The law was enacted twenty years later, although until the 1880s it met with substantial resistance, including armed clashes between the citizenry and enforcing militia.

Alexis de Tocqueville wrote in 1830 that "Americans are infinitely better educated than any other place in the world." Part of the evidence for this was the success of the school textbooks and dictionaries written by Noah Webster. *The American Speller* and the *Elementary Spelling Book* sold fifteen million copies by 1837. The purpose of his American spellers and dictionaries was again political, to create a national language, distinct from British, that would unify the new nation.

Yet at the same time that the political shift was occurring between England and America, both countries were also evolving from an agricultural to an industrial economy. The emphasis on a utilitarian education taught in a common language suited, and was reinforced by, America's emerging industrial economy. The common or public school, which taught reading, arithmetic, and citizenship, was an instrument first of Americanization and second of industrialization. Utilitarian goals took their place alongside civil and patriotic aims as the changes from colony to fledgling republic to industrial nation gradually occurred.

Industrialization also produced social changes that weakened the educative role of the family and posed further threats to older forms of religious schooling. Sunday schools, for example, were created because of extensive child labor. Since most children had to work twelve hours a day, their only time for schooling was on Sundays, when factories, mines, and mills were idle. Early Sunday schools taught reading, writing, and religion. When child labor laws were enacted, Sunday schools left the reading and writing to public schools and concentrated exclusively on religious teaching.

By the late nineteenth century, in their attempt to limit the spread of Catholicism from large waves of new immigrants, state control of education was supported actively by mainstream Protestant churches that had once opposed it. Methodists, Baptists, Presbyterians, and Congregationalists hoped to instill generalized Protestant values of hard work, frugality, and respect for both private and public property into secular schools that would be attended by children of Catholic immigrants.

In sum, the changing responsibility for education was largely a reflection of a changing society. When society's needs shifted, responsibility for education likewise shifted. It lay with family and church in colonial times and moved to civil authorities after independence from Britain. In agrarian America education was not thought of as a discrete segment of society. Nor was it truly a part of the monetary economy or a matter of political concern and public consciousness until the emergence of the industrial era, when it was supported by tax dollars that were measured and accounted for. The one-room schoolhouse had been displaced by the statehouse, and public education grew like crazy.

"It's Déjà Vu All Over Again"

Boston opened the nation's first publicly supported high school in 1821, and in 1852 Massachusetts passed the first compulsory school-attendance law in the United States. Many people believed that the use of taxes to support secondary schools was unlawful. The disagreement was settled in 1874, when the Michigan Supreme Court ruled that publicly supported high schools were legal. State after state then passed laws mandating that taxes be used to support a public school system of elementary, secondary, and even postsecondary schools. Every state had such a law by 1918, thus consolidating a process that had begun a hundred years before and ensuring government's control and responsibility for education.

The most significant education act of the nineteenth century was the federal Morrill Act of 1862, which established land-grant colleges and universities to "teach such branches of learning as are related to agriculture and the mechanic arts." In the middle of the Civil War, Congress granted the states huge tracts of land to sell, in order to finance the building of agricultural and technical colleges and universities. Proceeds from the sale of over 17.4 million acres of land went to finance developments in public education.

The Morrill Act fused the interests of government, education, and the farming community into a national policy, and it led to the establishment of agricultural extension programs, the mechanization of agriculture, and the birth of modern farming in the United States. Between 1855 and 1895, for example, the hourly labor required to produce one bushel of corn declined from four hours and thirty-four minutes to forty-one minutes, and, between 1830 and 1894 the equivalent wheat production time declined from over three hours to only ten minutes. Perhaps the most impressive legacy born of the Morrill Act was the understanding that education, open to all and focused on learning applicable to real economic needs, could not be divorced from economic growth and national strategy. It is a lesson we need to relearn today.

By contrast, a lesson that we know all too well is that government is often very late meeting market needs, and once it has met a need, it does not step aside. Ironically, the land-grant act established the highly successful agricultural extension program just as America's agricultural economy was drawing to a close. Public spending on agricultural extension programs today is $1.4 billion compared to the about $80 million spent on industrial extension programs, even though agricultural producers contribute about 2 percent to the GNP compared to manufacturers' 18 percent. Worse still, there are *no* educational extension programs at all to support the remaining 80 percent in services or information jobs, except for some extension studies in nursing and education.

However nobly we may interpret the land-grant act today, its main purpose originally was political. With the country in the middle of the Civil War, education reform was not exactly a topic on the front burner. The act may have bribed western and border states to stay in the Union, and after the Civil War it assuaged and enticed the South to accept rejoining the Union. The major incentives for educational change were thus political rather than economic.

Nevertheless, when the politics of national unity coincided with the politics of economic development in America, significant advances occurred in education. Today the politics of unity focus on racial equality and elimination of class distinction. The politics of economic development, on the other hand, focus on international trade, global competition, and jobs. The two are not aligned, and that is why political action is not moving education into the twenty-first century.

Why is education one of the few remaining institutions that is national, rather than international, in scope? The reason, again, is that educational institutions are generally shaped by social and political forces rather than economic concerns. Every country has used education to promote national unity. Bismarck, in particular, developed the Prussian education system because of the need to unify German principalities. Colonial powers used it to override ethnic and tribal loyalties. Education is now governed by just the opposite logic—to revive these loyalties and often instill social and political rivalries. Had the motive force of educational development been economic, schools would have evolved globally along with the current shift to a global economy.

The most significant governmental education act of the twentieth century was the GI Bill of Rights. Like the Morrill Act, it came in response to war, stimulated more by social and political change than by economic and technological conditions. The federal government has often justified changes in educational policy on the basis of military needs. Since its inception in 1944, the GI Bill has either paid or lent money to veterans of World War II, the Korean War, and the Vietnam War. It has been the single largest educational initiative in the United States, with over $140 billion in grants or loans and a total of seventeen million college-bound recipients.

The GI Bill, however, benefited veterans' personal lives after they left the service more than it affected our military preparedness. It was intended to repay our debt to those who defended the country, not to direct their study into areas that would secure our national defense. The GI of the forties became the "man in the gray flannel suit" of the fifties. And the education that veterans received, again ironically, was designed largely to meet the needs of an industrial economy that was even then on the wane.

The launching of *Sputnik* in 1957 marked the end of the industrial era and the beginning of the information economy. The country instantly became gripped by the Soviet threat to our national security and saw education in science, math, and engineering as an important way to counter it. Relying on past political rallying calls, the government responded with the National

Defense Education Act of 1958. The military-industrial complex powered the economy, and education was more captive to government defense initiatives than it was responsive to larger market needs.

The next sign that government-run education was faltering and continuing to ignore market needs came in 1983, when a blue-ribbon government panel known as the National Commission on Excellence in Education issued the widely quoted report, *A Nation at Risk*. Again pushing political hot buttons, the report cited national defense, not the economy and technology, as reasons to act. "If an unfriendly foreign power had attempted to impose on America the mediocre educational performance that exists today," it said, "we might well have viewed it as an act of war."[2]

Thus, political forces have dominated American education reform for more than two centuries, sometimes mandating reform to address issues of national unity, sometimes responding to concerns about national defense. In either event, education initiatives served the needs of the state. Historically economic growth and productivity were never the major cause of systemic change in education.

Today the civil servants in the education establishment are on the defensive, trying to hold on to their dominant role, but they are no longer able to couch educational reform and the mission of schools in terms of national defense and responsible citizenship and ignore the needs of individuals concerned about their jobs and of companies concerned about global competition. With the demise of the Soviet Union, education's mission is hardly preparation for war.

THIS TIME THE MOTIVATION IS ECONOMIC

"History doesn't repeat itself," said Mark Twain. "At best it sometimes rhymes." The last shift in the forces driving education was from religious to political; this time it is from political to economic.

The values missing from the government-dominated educational system that the business-led replacement will more likely institute are not related to greater social or political equality. The missing values are fundamentally economic. They are about our pocketbooks and how to restore our intergenerational rise in living standards. They are about keeping the American dream from becoming a nightmare.

The establishment of business values in our educational systems addresses the need to revive our economic leadership. The free market brought down communist and socialist governments around the world and is likely to bring down the hegemony of government-directed education. Maintaining any developed country's high standard of living will mean an emphasis on economic values over social and political ones. Future business dominance of the educating function, therefore, will emphasize values such as competition, service, and standards.

When all the universities in Texas combined graduate two people qualified to teach calculus but more than five hundred trained to coach football, it is an indication that values of social consumption have crushed values of economic production. The calculus/coach ratio can be taken as a measure of market demand. If government presses for a new ratio, and all that it implies, it is interpreted as an attempt to regulate education and not allow the free market to operate. If business presses for a new ratio, however, it is interpreted as an attempt to protect our economic future.

The effort to redirect education toward math, science, and technology is guiding the educational marketplace, whether it is made by government or by business. Its goal is to redefine basic values and recapture a high standard of living, irrespective of the difference between free versus regulated educational markets.

The private sector doesn't want to take over the public schools. It wants an education system that supplies the necessary human skills to keep the economy and society healthy. The current system does not do that. It was built to serve an economy and society that no longer exist. The new ways of learning and educating for the future are evolving right now. There are roles for everyone to play—executives, educators, government, and the public—and they are very different from previous roles. The pace of technological change is transforming everyone, not just students, into learners, and it is pushing our economic institutions to become educators.

Since personal computers hit the market in 1981, for example, a third of U.S. households have at least one,[3] and more than sixty million people have learned to operate them. Although some commercial schools and some progressive elementary and secondary schools teach computing, most of those sixty million people learned computing in other ways, outside of school. In addition to trial and error, these included self-teaching from manuals; watching neighbors or other "coaches," videos distributed by software vendors, and learning channels on television; and utilizing tutorials that software programs routinely have built into them. Computers linking interactively with television to produce edutainment will experience similar growth and require similar training in the future. This, too, is likely to take place outside the classroom.

Educating employees has also become a big business. Members of the baby boom generation have long since left schools and campuses, where growth is now flat or negative, and are employed in the workplace, where they continue learning, now more work related, through their business rather than the government.

While this increase in consumer and employee education is taking place, there is also a parallel increase in the number of businesses helping existing school systems. There are, for example, over 140,000 business-education partnerships. Most are philanthropic and create good public relations, and while a small number of these programs are creative and successful, even the best do not spread systemically or transform how the nation's students learn. Nearly one out of two schools depend on private companies to make up for budgetary shortfalls created by government cutbacks. Both business and society are serving their mutual interests by endeavoring to upgrade student education in order to head off a perceived shortage of qualified labor.

Ironically, when it comes to education business is more aware of its supportive role as a reformer than of its leadership role as a revolutionary. As a reformer helping students, teachers, and schools, its efforts may serve to patch up a failed, existing public system. But they are largely demonstrations of good corporate citizenship and are only indirectly related to the basic purpose of enterprise. That purpose is the provision of goods and services to meet market needs, and it is in carrying out this task that, without even knowing it, business will revolutionize learning.

The major reason is that the business community, not the education establishment, must embrace new technologies to survive. Computers, telecommunications, and consumer electronics have become the infrastructure technologies of this economy. And whichever sectors of society take them up, they profoundly alter the way we learn. To an extraordinary degree, business has taken them up, but education has not. Crumbling institutions rarely embrace new technologies as a means to revive themselves. But those institutions that do adopt new technologies will transform how learning takes place for those within their ranks and those they reach outside.

At first these revolutions in learning will have indirect, even unintended, consequences. Businesses simply need to keep up-to-date with the necessary tools of value-creation and management. The economic value they add to the marketplace derives increasingly from these technologies, and more and more of that value is related to service, information, knowledge, and learning. Thus, ever so slowly, enterprise becomes educator, largely unaware of this new role, not wanting it, not thinking of itself this way, and certainly not crowning itself as inheritor of it. Meanwhile, people begin to learn more outside of schools than in, and as schools lose their monopoly over "schooling," they become less and less relevant to our lives. Nevertheless, the need for learning and education continues, and the participants expand beyond students and teachers to new players, this time in the business community, which sparked the revolution in the first place.

Today a few businesses emphasize the importance of phrases

like "smart products," "machine intelligence," "interactive learning systems," and "knowledge-based enterprise." Remember, it
took one or two decades for "data-base" to become "database," for
the term to move from technical jargon to common speech.
Knowledge-based products and services today are still described
in cobbled phrases, but as they become more familiar to us
through time, they too will lose their strangeness and become
more commonplace, a part of the natural way things are done.
When that happens, companies will refer to themselves intentionally as in the knowledge business—sure, isn't everyone?—the
way 90 percent of the economy today is in the service business.

Business's freedom of action is limited to how, not whether, it
will respond to the challenge of educating. Just as government
took over the lead from church and family, business will become
heir to the lead at this next historical turn. But it is a very reluctant heir.

Business will not assume the lead by usurping the role of
director of the nation's public schools. It does not wish or seek to
inherit this public trust. Instead, overlapping with the declining
public school system, it is almost unintentionally evolving new
meanings for learning and new methods for delivering education.
And it is doing so in ways that are consistent with its fundamental
role as business, competitively fulfilling unmet needs in the marketplace. All business visions are anchored in this fundamental
belief.

In our economic system, we believe that competition is good
because it keeps the players active in their search for new and
better ways to provide goods and services. When success leads to
an overwhelming market share, however, a culture emerges that
is arrogant, self-satisfied, inward-looking, and unaware of threatening change. The same is true with regard to competition among
sectors of society for predominance in education. When church
and state were competitors, each had to vie to demonstrate its
greater ability to meet society's needs. But now that the state has
a virtual monopoly, it has become less responsive to those needs.
Had it been subject to the rigors of competition and the demands

of the marketplace, it might have retained its social and economic relevance.

VALUES DETERMINE WHICH PROBLEMS ARE ADDRESSED

Each institution bearing the mantle of education takes values, beliefs, and practices that are instrumental to its own success and applies them to education. The particular traits of successive leaders of learning define anew, in what they teach, the problems society deems most critical. Often their solutions are not a panacea but a best choice. Their efforts do not solve all educational problems so much as determine which old problems to chose to solve, which ones to continue to live with, and which new ones to contend with later. In their wake these efforts create other problems, dimly perceived but accepted at the time as unimportant. Meanwhile, completely new problems are unwittingly generated that are scarcely considered. The results are neither all good nor entirely bad.

Religious dominance of education in colonial times emphasized such values as learning to live according to God's will. The results included Quaker toleration as well as Puritan intolerance. Family-based educational values in agrarian America strengthened the extended family. To be a good Christian and to honor thy father and mother were among the values that were explicitly articulated in the classroom. But such values also established a righteous foundation for disregarding the social and ethnic values of "other" groups outside the family circle.

In the interest of forging a union of many competing religious groups, the Founding Fathers emphasized separation of church and state, and schools slowly dropped teaching all but the most basic social values. As with church-dominated education, the government-run variety also installed its own practices. School was "democratized"—open to all; school boards were duly elected; and teaching was a public service rather than a service to God. Loyalty was redefined as "good citizenship" rather than "service to God." School became compulsory because democracy required a knowledgeable citizenry. Student government, while not required, was commonly found in public high schools; but there is no comparable "student church" in church-run schools, and it remains to be seen whether there will be anything like "student business" in business-led education.

Government's lead in education stressed the need to produce literacy and mathematical competence for large numbers of people, to serve both economic and political needs. But it also weakened religious and family values and fostered an educational democracy based on the lowest common denominator.

Government, like the churches before, brought in a kaleidoscope of funding policies and problems. Because of the politics of states' rights and local autonomy, public schools were funded largely by property taxes, a practice that meant wealthy suburbs where property values were high could afford well-funded schools. By contrast, inner cities—where property values were relatively low and demands for other social services were high—were grossly underfunded. This American peculiarity of funding schools locally would seem at odds with democratic ideals of equal treatment, and it created a two-tiered school system in which the quality of education was linked to factors such as race and wealth. School systems in most developed countries are funded from taxes levied nationally.

With the *Brown* v. *Board of Education* decision in 1954, the government-run school system became the major institution used in the struggle for racial integration. In doing so, it seemed to experience a shift in core values from learning to social justice and the resolution of social conflict. "Putting social ends ahead of the goal of learning," Peter Drucker argues, "became a major factor in the decline of American basic education."[4]

In a learning system dominated by business, a key question will be whether its values and practices—such as the need to integrate a workforce increasingly diversified by race, gender, and national origin—will lead to greater success than the government has had in its attempts to legally enforce integration. Or will business-led education shortchange the needy, favor the white-collar class, and further skew our social structure, creating a have and have-not nation with a shrunken middle?

If there is reason for hope here, it will not be because business has a more liberal social policy than government, but because demography requires social integration in business. And businesses understand that. They pay attention to the bilingual and multiethnic labor force, the two-income family, the graying of America, and other demographic trends that are transforming our labor force and our marketplace. They do not try to hold back demographic shifts; they try to prepare for them.

Business, therefore, will educate minorities. To be sure, it will do so more for its own good than for the larger social good, but the effect will be much the same. If students leave school unable to read and use math, business will teach them what they lack. It will do so, not to improve ghetto life, but because it needs competent workers to sustain good corporate performance. Acting out of self-concern, business will very probably redress our social concerns no less adequately than church and government have done.

As business becomes more influential in setting educational objectives, we will get a strong dose of business values. A debate about these values and the purpose they serve will inevitably follow, centered around the question of which ones will be acceptable and which not. Because the new is always suspect, many business values will not be welcomed as they enter the educational world. Will they bring a focus on profit and materialism, as many critics of business fear? Will they bring a concern for self-development and sustainable growth, as many proponents hope?

Another debate will focus on the distinction between moral and practical learning. There has always been a division between those who see education as the repository and training ground for our moral values and those who emphasize the practical reasons for education, such as supplying a labor force that is prepared for the requirements of enterprise and economic health. The former include many humanists, ministers, voting citizens, democratic

leaders, and members of the professional educational establishment. The business community has always been the primary
spokesperson for emphasis on the latter.

This debate ebbs and flows, as though we could select between
the alternatives, as though, if we made up our minds, we could
direct education one way or the other. We don't quite have that
much choice. Historical forces will not anoint one the winner and
the other the loser. What will happen is that, as when any institution takes an increasingly dominant role in education, the values it represents will gain greater emphasis, while the values of
the institutions whose educational role is shrinking will become
less dominant. Just as church-based education emphasizes morality, for example, enterprise-based education emphasizes practicality. As corporations take on more and more of the educating
role, the thrust of that education will be oriented toward their
needs, which are more practical than moral.

This doesn't mean that education will cease to emphasize hu-
manistic, political, and moral values. It means that these values
will be addressed by more specialized players in the educational
arena. Private religious schools, for example, maintain a high
degree of morally based education, and they tend to deliver it
with better quality than any other educating institution. Similarly,
in the long-term future, government-based education has an opportunity to pick up the educational market segments or functions to which it, not business, is particularly suited, such as
regulation and national standards. Preparedness to earn a living is
something that business knows more about.

Since the teaching of moral values has long been the province
of the church, church educators are often surprised to discover
that corporations devote more time to values education than public schools do. Business, too, is intensely interested in values and
deals with them in employee education. Thus business-driven
learning does not mean less moral and ethical education than
under government-led learning. There are good and bad models
for a moral education in all walks of life, and we wouldn't want
such courses taught by Ivan Boesky and Michael Milken any more
than by Richard Nixon and Alan Cranston.

Here is a contemporary example of how enterprise-based education blends morality and practicality, taken from the "Values Challenge Taker" program developed for DuPont.

You are the senior environmental engineer at one of our plant sites. A serious process problem has developed that will increase the discharge of toxic effluent. This increase is above your targeted operating level and will impact the environment to a degree, but it is within regulatory limits. The problem can be fixed now with a two-day shutdown and lost production, or it can be done at the next scheduled shutdown in three months' time. Do you

(a) live with it for three months?
(b) shut down and fix it now?
(c) pass on the information and let someone else decide?
(d) shape the facts to minimize the concern of others?

Here's another question raised in values education; it will be familiar to women executives. On occasion you and your manager travel together on business. During one of these trips, after an evening of cocktails, he makes a pass at you in the elevator. He has never made any kind of advance to you in the past. You

(a) suggest he's had too much to drink and just forget it.
(b) report him to his manager.
(c) tell him if he doesn't cut it out, you'll report him.
(d) ignore it because, since he didn't threaten your job, you have no right to complain.
(e) say "Thanks, but no thanks."

The danger in a business-led learning revolution is not that practical education will eliminate education about values; the real danger lies in the future of an economic underclass that has already grown to alarming proportions, despite the efforts of government programs such as busing to overcome segregation, welfare to overcome poverty, and school lunch programs to combat malnutrition. A major challenge for business is not whether it will cut or increase funding for these social goals, but whether it can invent alternative solutions to problems that threaten to undermine its own success. Smart products will not sell to dumb consumers; worker training programs will not take illiterate new hires.

One future possibility is that government-run schools will focus on becoming the high-volume, low-cost producer of excellent basic education. Its market then will be the underclass that the private sector will gladly leave to it as the least attractive end of education from a business perspective. From a social perspective, however, the worst thing that business could do is abandon public sector education to this fate.

The best thing it can do is help public education use all the tools and techniques of the information economy so that it can provide the excellent basic education necessary to business and to society as a whole. These tools and techniques must also be used in education by government, church, family, and the individual to provide a vital new life for public education, a share in the schoolhouse of the future. We cannot afford a third-world country inside our country. Neither can we afford a third-rate education system pinning us down.

CHAPTER 2

FOUR STEPS TO
WISDOM

Where is the Life we have lost in living?
Where is the wisdom we have lost in knowledge?
Where is the knowledge we have lost in information?

—T. S. Eliot, Choruses from "The Rock," I
Collected Poems 1909–1919

During a business trip to Asia, an educated executive from the Western world visited a wise Zen master. When he arrived, the master asked him what he wanted, and the visitor replied that he wanted to learn how to achieve wisdom. The master nodded, lifted a teapot, and poured its contents into the executive's tiny cup. The cup soon overflowed, and the master kept pouring until the pot was empty.

As with any great story, particularly a Zen story, this one has many meanings. One is that you must often *unlearn* before you can learn more. You have to empty your mind to make room for a new idea. For example, government-based education is not the only way to learn and grow, even though that notion has been ingrained in us all our lives. It's time to change that. We must unlearn this "truth" so that we can move ahead. Business-based education is another way. It has already begun. What does it look like?

It looks like a knowledge business, and any business can become one. To understand how, let's explore the "four steps to wisdom," the journey from basic to profound expressions of the world around us.

ANY BUSINESS CAN BECOME A KNOWLEDGE BUSINESS

Long before there were computers, T. S. Eliot linked information, knowledge, and wisdom in the poem that opens this chapter. Since then many people have fine-tuned this progression, added data (as in "Where is the information we have lost in data?"), and turned the sequence around from loss to gain.

The result is a four-step progression from data to information to knowledge to wisdom. Data are ways of expressing things, and information is the arrangement of data into meaningful patterns. Knowledge is the application and productive use of information, and wisdom, finally, is the discerning use of knowledge. Each step does not necessarily lead to the next, but they must be taken in proper sequence to achieve the final goal.

Data are the basic building blocks of the information economy and of a knowledge business. They are the way we express things and group them together. Or, as Robert Lucky, a former director of AT&T Bell Labs, says, they are the unorganized sludge of the information age. In this economy we focus on data that come to us in four particular forms: numbers, words, sounds, and images. And their functions, or what we do with them, include creating them, manipulating or processing them, moving them around, and storing them.

Random numbers are data; a random number table is information. Sounds can be thought of as notes (data) and, when arranged in some system, as music (information). Depending upon the skill of the composer and performer, the result can be greater knowledge, or even wisdom, for those who listen and learn. In mathematics the building blocks are numbers, and through processes like addition, subtraction, multiplication, and division, we create meaningful patterns of information. Algebra and geometry organize the information into bodies of knowledge. In language the building blocks include nouns, verbs, adjectives, and adverbs, or (more generally) words that, when arranged in meaningful patterns, become information. These in turn may take the form of literature from which knowledge and wisdom may stem.

As they apply to the economy, data, information, and knowledge have life cycles, and such cycles are usefully divided into four quarters: gestation (Q1), growth (Q2), maturity (Q3), and decline (Q4). Data's economic importance was embryonic in the 1950s and 1960s and entered a growth quarter in the 1970s and 1980s. In the third quarter of the cycle, data are now a commodity. In the fourth quarter of the cycle, a few decades from now, data will become a utility like gas or electricity, which you simply plug into and are charged for usage.

Information is a quarter turn after data in life cycle progressions. Its economic importance was recognized only about a decade ago, and it is still in the growth phase of its cycle. One day it too will mature. What will take its place? Behind it in the queue, gestating right now, is knowledge. The economic importance of knowledge is still in the first quarter of its life cycle, poised for takeoff and accelerated growth in the years immediately ahead.

An intuitive way to appreciate the difference between information and knowledge is to substitute the word *data* every time you see, hear, write, or speak the word *information*. Chances are that there will be an emotional resistance. It won't feel right. It's going backward, and it strikes us against the grain. In business, for example, *chief information officers* are much bigger wheels than *data processors*. The latter aren't even officers. Data now are widgets, commodities, just not as powerful or prestigious as the information derived from them.

Within a decade we will feel the same kind of resistance in

talking about information and information-based tools. Knowledge and knowledge-based tools will have greater power and appeal. Information-based products and services will have lost a lot of their buzz, not because they were a fad, but because they will have been superseded by a more powerful and useful generation of offerings. The value of knowledge will supersede the value of information, just as the value of information took over from a focus on data.

We are only beginning to understand what the knowledge age is all about. We do know that future growth for mature businesses comes from advancing level by level, from data through information to knowledge, and that any business can transform itself into a knowledge business. Furthermore, any business offering knowledge-based products and services, whether it realizes it or not, becomes a learning business. The business itself must continually learn how to provide that product or service, and customers become learners through the use of knowledge-based products and services. Knowledge businesses are not limited to brainy folks in education, to nerdy folks in "high tech," or even to any folks who employ only smart people and sell only to smart customers. Rather, every business has the potential to become a knowledge business, one whose greatest value is derived from the knowledge that has become an intrinsic part of its offering to the marketplace.

Every consumer also has the potential to become a lifelong learner. The provider implicitly says to the customer, "You get smarter when you use my product, because you not only get the thing itself, but you also learn how to use it in a more powerful and enjoyable way than its pre-knowledge-based ancestor. My product educates while it serves."

In the world of business, words like "information," "knowledge," "education," and "learning" are often used interchangeably and without definition. While "education" has been badly pilloried in the past few years, "knowledge" and "learning" are currently positive and popular. We hear phrases like a "knowledge worker" and "learning organization," but they have been used so facilely and superficially that they almost lose their meaning.

Buzzwords produce muddy thinking, and in reality there is a significant difference in the meaning of the words *education* and *learning* as they relate to the four steps to wisdom and to business.

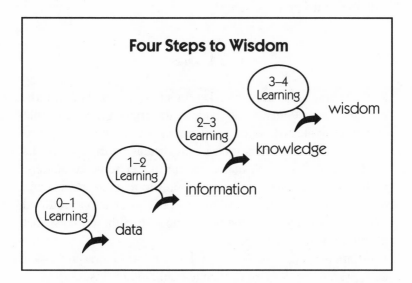

In the four steps to wisdom, *education* is instruction and mastery at a given step or level, and *learning* is the movement from one level to the next. Schools teach education more than they teach learning. Businesses have to avoid this trap. To serve as an information or knowledge business that will educate its customers, a company must first learn, then enable its customers to learn, in successive steps.

Each step up in learning requires a new technology platform. Computers enabled us to take what might be called the "0–1 Learning" step up and ushered in the data age. They required lots of training, and thousands of people used them. The marriage of computers and telecommunications was the basis for the "1–2 Learning" step up from data to information, and it brought us into the information era. By this stage computers required relatively little training, and millions of people used them.

The technology platform that will make possible the "2–3 Learning" step up and usher in the knowledge age is the blending of computers and telecommunications with human actions. By the time the knowledge phase matures, around a decade from now, billions of people will use computers with no training at all. Can we imagine the technology platform that will enable us to take the final step to wisdom?

1–2 LEARNING

Each of these steps must be taken in succession by both a business and its customers. For example, the original room-size IBM computers collected, sorted, and stored data in the "0–1 Learning" step, and customers utilized the data as information in the "1–2 Learning" step. With the advent of electronic computers, that process became much more sophisticated and much more useful—so valuable that in some cases the information produced by a business often became worth more than the business that produced it in the first place.

Computer-generated airline guides and reservation systems, for example, are often more profitable than airlines. Insurance on a rented car can cost and earn more than the car rental. It can be cheaper to dig for oil on Wall Street than in the ground. These are all examples of information-based activities that often present better economic opportunities than the businesses that originally generated the information.

The airline industry sustained $8 billion in losses during the first two years of this decade, and AMR Corporation alone lost $1.22 billion of that. Without its American Airlines operations, however, AMR would have been profitable. In 1992 its information-intensive, nonairline businesses generated $240 million in operating profits on $1.7 billion in revenues. The company strategy in the 1980s was to grow the airline aggressively, but overcapacity, fare wars, and volatile fuel prices have caused AMR to reverse this strategy. Now it is shrinking the airline, dumping competitive short-hop routes, and building its information businesses around activities related to the airline industry. It does this in the belief that diversifying its information businesses is worth more than the declining original business.

The most important of these information businesses is the Sabre travel reservation system, the world's largest privately owned, real-time computer network. Instead of keeping it proprietary, the AMR offered it to all airlines and established it as an industry standard. Now it has used its expertise from Sabre to diversify into myriad other information activities. It has retrained ticket processors at its key-punch center in Barbados, for example, to handle medical and insurance claims for Travelers Corporation and Blue Cross/Blue Shield. AMR is managing the Warsaw airport for the Polish government, training Russian computer programmers at Aeroflot in new reservations software, and building reservations and pricing systems for the French railroad and the "Chunnel," the tunnel under the English Channel. It bought a $195 million piece of Canadian Airlines to get a twenty-year, $2 billion contract providing reservations, accounting, data-processing, and pricing services.

Informationalized businesses become something quite different and more valuable than the original businesses from which the information was generated. When the process first begins, the information doesn't seem so amazing; it is just a part or a by-product of the core business. Through a process that takes some years, the importance of the information increases and increases. The value added from the information content slowly comes to be worth more than the original "thing" itself, and the information stage shifts from growth to maturity. This is where we are now, on the cusp of the "2–3 Learning" step up, moving beyond information to knowledge.

2–3 LEARNING

In a business, what begins incrementally, as a matter of degree, may at a certain time become different in kind. There are two parallel developments: the evolution of the business into something other than what it was; and the realization of this shift by those involved. Sometimes the shift is recognized only after the fact. The informationalization of businesses, for example, seemed to occur before it was generally recognized as such. The opposite also occurs. As business begins to take the next step in the learning progression, it is quite likely that "knowledge" will become popular and sought after very quickly, even before it becomes widespread or its importance widely recognized.

If this happens, awareness of the value of knowledge will probably exceed a business's ability to extract it from the particular setting it is embedded in. What is the knowledge value in a pair of socks, a home mortgage, an electric bill, or a foreign exchange credit? For some, "knowledge" will become a buzzword, and because it has more cachet than the already too familiar word *information,* many people in business will start using it indiscriminately. For others it will bring as much power as data and information brought in their turn, ultimately redefining the very business they are in.

Whether a new concept is just a buzzword or truly describes a major shift in the source of economic value depends, not on its popularity, but first on the power of the technology platform upon which it is built. The platform that is now emerging is very powerful. The merger of computers, telecommunications, consumer electronics, publishing, and entertainment is the economic equivalent of geological plate tectonics. Industries instead of continents are bumping up against each other, and knowledge is the volcanic lava liberated from their merging and blending. We are experiencing nothing short of a revolution in learning and the knowledge business. This is not a fad: this will cause major changes in our economy and our society.

Many simple, minor changes occur on and under the surface long before a volcano finally erupts and gets everyone's attention. Knowledge certainly existed before we ever had an information economy, so how did it manifest itself in pre–information age goods and services? And how will the new technologies amplify the knowledge dimension of these goods?

GET SMART

Knowledge is information put to productive use. In a product this can be as simple and mundane as the pop-up button that tells you when the turkey is cooked. If the button comes with the oven, rather than with the turkey, it can also turn itself off and sound a buzzer. Knowledge is in a tennis racket that glows where the ball strikes it, to help correct the stroke. It is in a diaper that changes color when it is wet. All are examples of products that take information about what is happening to them and communicate it to the consumer in a practical way. They are not earth-shattering products. Each of them gives more value, however, than its preknowledge predecessor.

Intelligence evolved slowly, both in people and in products. Comedian George Carlin once wondered about the Thermos: "When you pour in cold water it stays cold," he said, "and when you pour in hot water it stays hot. How does it know which to do?"[1] This question in jest is actually at the heart of the matter: How do products know?

We have long been accustomed to refrigerators that "know" when to defrost. The simple home thermostat, which senses room temperature and then calls for heating or cooling, is a pre–computer age smart product. It's one of the simplest forms of stimulus and response and often cited by researchers in learning theory. Thermostats today are even smarter. They can be programmed to vary by time and day, and they can be tied to the security system to sense fire and intruders. In other words, smart products adjust to changing circumstances.

Another smart product is a micro-PCM, or phase-change material. When the cloth of a micro-PCM ski jacket senses cold, it turns warm. The same micro-PCMs can be embedded in car seats, curtains, insulation materials, and wallpaper.

Cloud Gel, produced by Suntek in Albuquerque, is a new material that can prevent overheating when applied to window glass. When the sun is strong or the temperature goes above a specified level, Cloud Gel reflects rather than transmits 90 percent of the sun's rays over a difference of three degrees Fahrenheit. Thus at sixty-eight degrees, a treated window or skylight lets in more warmth, but at seventy-one degrees it starts to bounce radiant heat back into the atmosphere. If all the world's annual six billion square feet of new glass used the product, energy consumption would drop by 17 percent, and over a billion tons of air pollution would be eliminated.

These are examples of knowledge that is built into the product itself. Intelligence might be built in at the atomic or molecular level, such as in chemicals that are noxious or harmful. Molecular structures that are engineered to biodegrade when they reach a dangerous stage are smart products. Knowledge can also be built in as tiny chips and transmitters in a variety of products such as home appliances, vending machines, railroad cars, or elevators. This is what happens when the Otis service agent shows up to fix elevator number eight in a skyscraper, and the building manager says nothing is wrong with number eight. "Yes, but there's going to be," says the service agent, "and I'm here to prevent that." A machine that has sensors that automatically trip a reorder and shipment for a part it knows is about to break down also has built-in smarts. Xerox's field service system has a telephone built into some of its large machines that can connect to a modem and thus provide data for preventive maintenance.

Smart products are usually described as futuristic computers that think. "By the year 2030," says the director of the Mobile Robot Laboratory at Carnegie Mellon University, "compact, PC-like machines will be able to reason, perceive, and act upon their environment with full human equivalence." Futuristic statements like these obscure the fact that smart products already exist and are in widespread use.

Automobile tires, for example, tend to lose air and wear unevenly, reducing performance and gobbling gas. Goodyear's "smart tire" contains a microchip that collects and analyzes tire data, then tells the driver, "I'm low on air, time for a pit stop," or, "I'm wearing thin on my right side, time for a realignment." The first part of the message conveys information, the second tells you what to do, the knowledge component. It's up to you to make the wise move.

AAA Triptiks provide information about highways, hotels, and hot spots on your route, and General Motors is preparing to deliver this information electronically to your car, in real time. Useful information becomes more valuable when you can act on it instantly. The beginning and end points of your trip are data, and using them, the routing service can provide you with valuable information. Armed with that information, you are in the know. And the knowledge is increased if it is updated electronically with real-time traffic reports and displayed on a dashboard screen. It's up to the driver to have the wisdom to take the suggested detour, wait out the traffic jam, or stop for dinner. Can you ask the Triptik questions? Can the Triptik get information that it didn't have before the questions were asked? The more useful and relevant the Triptik is to the journey as it happens, the more it becomes a knowledge product.

Another characteristic of knowledge products is that *the more you use them, the smarter they get.* The Baldrige Award–winning Ritz-Carlton Hotel chain is putting in a knowledge-based system that tracks customers' particular preferences and needs and automatically provides them anywhere in the worldwide system. If a customer in Boston requests six hypoallergenic pillows and six boxes of tissues for his room, the next time he checks into a Ritz-Carlton Hotel in Hong Kong or Hawaii, they'll be in those rooms too, when he gets there. Information systems can log customers' idiosyncratic preferences. Knowledge-based systems combine information with human action and monitor the outcomes.

If you want to get your car checked, CAMS, the Computer Aided Maintenance System from General Motors, is a knowledge-based service that can help you. Designed initially to allow novice mechanics to diagnose and repair cars, it has evolved into something more: it has become a trainer for mechanics, enabling them to develop their own expertise repairing new electronics-based auto engines. Since all the CAMS terminals in garages are interconnected to a central database, each mechanic is the beneficiary of the combined skills of all the mechanics on the system. So the system gets smarter the more it is used. CAMS teaches a person how to become a good mechanic, and good mechanics teach the system how to become a better teacher. The more the product is used, the smarter *both* the product and the user become and the better the service is for the customer.

Some consumers, like students, learn more from the same product than others, and like teachers, some products instruct better than others. All smart products and services will have an increasing learning and knowledge component, and this will give them advantages over their nonintelligent cousins. Similarly, those who use them will be at an advantage over those who don't. Smart consumers using smart products and services are to be recognized as a huge segment in the knowledge marketplace.

When we say someone or something is intelligent, we mean that he, she, or it has the capacity for knowledge and for understanding novel situations. They comprehend information in ways that guide their actions and performance. Products increasingly display intelligence, and the people who use them benefit and often add to their own knowledge and intelligence.

Apart from the paradox of using more complicated things to make our lives simpler, the consumer learns more from using them. What makes the consumer smarter? Calculators were not allowed in classrooms when they were first introduced, even though they gave faster and more accurate results, because it was said that students who used them would no longer learn the underlying principles of calculation. The debate lasted about a decade. Although the greater utility of calculators was recognized immediately, it was only when the higher performance platform and subsequent greater learning became manifest that the resistance evaporated. What works wins.

Whereas drivers once needed to learn what was under the

hoods of their cars, today they don't particularly know or care. Their gain is the larger world that is available to them for having and driving the car, even though they do not know the car's underlying technology. Similarly, people who use knowledge-based products will not need to understand how they work. The use of a new technology enables people to learn and to be more knowledgeable whether they understand the underlying principles or not.

People are always interested in what a new technology will do for them and in how easy it will be to learn and use. That is why entertainment is often an important component of smart products. Video games are, of course, entertainment. But a videotape of cartoon characters installing an appliance is both entertaining and useful. Smart products and entertaining products increase learning more than dumb, boring ones, and this is why "infotainment" is often part of the blend of knowledge-based products and services.

Smart products did not exist in great abundance before the information era. Today they are relatively common, even if they are generally thought of as high-tech. What happens when even the most ordinary product learns to be smart? An economy of entirely smart products would be one that is more advanced than an economy of products that have no intrinsic ability to improve consumer performance. In the aggregate, the effect on society would be transformative, because in such an economy consumers of knowledge products (and not just the products themselves) become smarter with their use. Smart products and knowledge-based businesses create both smart consumers and a knowledgeable public. As employees, people will learn a living; as consumers they will become lifelong learners.

THE KNOWLEDGEBURGER

Any product can become a knowledge product, and any service can do the same. How, for example, could you turn a hamburger business into a knowledge business? Starting with the basic learning steps we outlined, let's first establish some basic hamburger data: its ingredients, for example, such as protein, fat, and carbohydrates, and their varying functions, such as nutrition, convenience, price, and aesthetic pleasure. When you put the data into a meaningful pattern, the information you derive tells you both the menu and the market—in other words, what business you are in.

The next step is to learn from the information, so that hamburgers become a knowledge business, and in addition to getting tasty and nutritional food, customers can make use of knowledge about that food. When customers place orders for an entire meal, for example, can the calorie and fat count be calculated and printed alongside the items on the bill, or even at the time of order, so they can make informed judgments about their order? What, then, is wisdom in the hamburger business? Perhaps in addition to taste and price, it is learning to eat the right food.

Can the same be done at a supermarket? When customers buy halibut steak, for example, they could flip electronically through a dozen recipes for halibut preparation, print one out, and pick up the additional ingredients at the same time. The knowledge here is *about* the product, rather than literally built into the product itself. Still, even a supermarket can add value by adding a learning component to the products it sells.

Selecting television programs can also become a learning experience. With over 100 channels now to choose from, and 500 to 1,500 on the way, viewers need to filter and select. Simply flipping channels is selecting from data. When these choices are organized into lists, as in *TV Guide,* they become information. If the program guide is listed on a television channel, shifted from paper to an electronic form of delivery, it is still an information-based product.

An interactive electronic program guide, however, would have the potential to become a knowledge product. If you do nothing more than control the speed with which the choices scroll in front of you, you are still using the guide only to get information. But once you can interact with the material being presented, you could put it to much more productive use. If you could ask for all the television programs this week that are comedies or are about pollution or cooking fish, then you have elevated the information to knowledge. The wise use of that knowledge is up to you.

When information can be sorted by any desirable criterion, you may use it to transform your television set into a learning device. It is then only another small leap to say, Why just a week? Why not all programs on pollution over a year or more? Why not smart filters that can scan past, present, and future programs for you, creating a video library on demand, according to the categories you select? And where will the smart filter be located, in the electronic television guide of the future or in the future television set itself? The resolution of such questions will bridge the gap between television and education as we have known them, making education and even entertainment into true knowledge businesses.

The Federal Communications Commission's 1992 decision to allow telephone companies to transmit television programming is making electronic program selection, and much more, a reality. The fiber-optic and/or wireless digital networks on which they run will not be in place for about a decade. When they are, both schools and businesses, students and consumers, will be able to roam through remote electronic libraries, offering everything from missed soap operas and movies to research references and medical files. Dialing up a video-service menu using the combined technologies of telephone, television, and computer blurs the distinction between consumer and learner.

Monthly bills can also be turned into knowledge products. Billing summaries, as for credit cards and telephone calls, can be pretty boring and confusing affairs. American Express was the first to distinguish itself from its competitors by separating a year's worth of customer transactions into categories useful for tax and business purposes. The individual charges are data, and the monthly bill is information, but a billing summary organized by category becomes a knowledge tool when it helps you control travel expenses and prepare your tax form.

Some credit card companies do this for a nominal fee at year end, but why not extend this with monthly and year-to-date displays as well? And while they are at it, why not offer a menu of other variables according to which the data can be displayed? Or for a one-time charge of five dollars, would you like your monthly bill to organize charges by category (food, travel, entertainment, and so on) rather than by date? How about in the format of your organization's travel and expense (T&E) reimbursement forms? Some knowledge businesses can be built around fee-based services that give customers choice about how information can best be put to productive use.

Knowledge products and services will have relatively short life cycles. It is hard to keep them proprietary. In commercial banks, for example, foreign exchange advisory services are very knowledge intensive. Wealthy clients often have global investment portfolios and need advice on how to handle the risks of hedging or speculating on their foreign exchange exposure. This kind of knowledge is subjective, and the ability to systematize it has not caught up with the rate of increase of knowledge on managing such risks. In some senses bankers want it that way, because high profit margins are associated with new knowledge. As you are able to make the knowledge systematic, the margins deteriorate.

Patent protections on intellectual property are still not nearly as developed as they are on "hard" technologies. So the half-life of proprietary information is short, unless you can find ways to build barriers around the knowledge built on top of the information. This is where advantages of scale enter in. If you are a big competitor, you probably know more about a market than the small players. The managerial challenge for those running foreign exchange advisory services, a knowledge-intensive business, is getting their professionals in New York, London, and Tokyo to share their knowledge. When that knowledge is systematized and widely shared, however, it will become available even to the small players.

When Business Becomes Educator, Consumers Become Learners

We speak of consumers as learners when they use intelligent products that both oblige them to learn and assist them in learning. All products and services have the potential to be smart, or intelligent, in this sense. Businesses will move in this direction because they will benefit by making their offerings smart. And when their customers use them, they will be engaged in a learning experience and an educational process.

To be sure, this is a far cry from the educational process of industrial era schooling. But it is equally certain that slowly, over the next two decades, businesses will come to think of their customers as learners and hence of themselves as educators. Their motives will be commercial, not altruistic. They will promote the learning experience for profit, and reciprocally, their customers will profit from that learning experience. This slice of the new education pie will use intelligent products the way earlier eras used the religious catechism and then the secular textbook.

Rap songs have replaced rapped knuckles as a means of learning important lessons, and multimedia makes the new catechism a lot more stimulating. Multimedia is the combination of words, sounds, and images, sent, displayed, and stored together in an electronic blend. Computer games and MTV music videos are examples of this intermingling of entertainment and education. These two powerful sectors of our economy will blend even further as multimedia and fiber-optic transmission mature. Entertainment may not become more educational, but education will certainly become more entertaining—particularly education as we have defined it, not limited to students and classrooms, but spread wide to a marketplace of lifelong learners.

A declining education system has the same opportunity as a declining business to reinvigorate and even redefine itself using the learning steps from data to information to knowledge. Too often, however, what state-run education teaches is not useful, not what students need to know. It has produced a generation of overtrained, underemployable college graduates filled with information they cannot put to productive use. When information is put to productive use, "2–3 Learning," the economic output is knowledge. From the perspective of what students need to know, business is often an even larger provider of such learning than schools, whether public or private. And consumers of any age become an even larger user of educational and learning activities and materials.

In the years ahead, people's use of knowledge-based products and services will be critical to their economic success. Learning will not be defined by the time, place, or institution that provides it, any more than by who does the learning. The value of one's education will be measured by its proportionate mix of data, information, and knowledge. The economic value of a business will be judged similarly. Businesses that can "informationalize" will do better than those that cannot. And those that know how to use a knowledge platform will be even more valuable and powerful than those that are just information-based.

Most companies have not yet transformed themselves into knowledge businesses; they are just beginning to grasp the concept and are looking for ways to act on it. As an individual, here's what you can do. Any time you find an example of a knowledge-based product or service, ask what it is doing differently from before. Then extract a principle and ask yourself how it could be applied in your own business.

For example, does your offering get better with use, adjust to changing circumstances, filter information and then put it to productive use, customize itself to individual preferences? Is it interactive? Each of these questions is worthy of consideration and discussion as a means of adding economic value to your business.

3–4 LEARNING: SO YOU WANT TO GET INTO THE WISDOM BUSINESS

The greatest part of the economic value of products and services today concerns information content. In the near future, as information is more systematized and becomes a commodity, growth and economic value will migrate to the knowledge component of these products and services. The technology platform for this reality is almost in place—and that raises the question of what comes after knowledge.

The comprehension of data, information, and knowledge is a rational process. When they have been around long enough, we may begin to treat them as truths. That is when they can become dogma, beliefs that somehow shouldn't be examined. We will have to ask if a particular piece of knowledge is dogma and question its veracity. To reach beyond knowledge to achieve wisdom, particularly as an economy and society rather than just as individuals, will require us to embrace and develop perspectives that call on intuition and emotion, on the nonrational.

That understanding is what caused Einstein to say that "imagination is more important than knowledge." In one of his famous thought experiments, Einstein asked what the world would look like if he could travel at the speed of light. This different perspective enabled him to transcend the current "knowledge" that time and space were absolutes and that light varied as it traveled through them. With this shift we redefined light as the absolute, and a space-time continuum became the new variable. Thus, Einstein's wisdom gave us new knowledge.

Paradoxically, however, wisdom is not what lies on the other side of what is known, because once we get there it becomes mere knowledge. The laws of relativity, for example, reside in the world of knowledge, while Einstein's imaginative shifts in perspective dwelt in the realm of wisdom.

Nothing on the near horizon suggests that economic value will soon be based on the "wisdom content" of products and services. What, in fact, is wisdom? Here is *Webster's* definition:

> Wisdom: . . . the ability to judge soundly and deal sagaciously with facts, especially as they relate to life and conduct; knowledge, with the capacity to make due use of it; perception of the best ends and the best means; discernment and judgment; . . .

Thus, all the necessary antecedents of wisdom—data, information, and knowledge—are already, or soon will be, in place. They are made available to us through increasingly sophisticated technologies and through knowledge-based products and services. Wisdom resides in the discernment, judgment, and perception with which these tools are used. Will there ever be wisdom-based goods and services, products in the marketplace that teach us to be wise? Perhaps the answer to that question—for businesses, schools, individuals, and society itself—lies in an eventual understanding of the most complex and sophisticated technology of all—the human brain. Until then, wisdom is that something always within our reach and ever so slightly beyond our grasp.

CHAPTER 3

THE CHATTER, THE STRING, AND THE CAN

How do you explain school to a higher intelligence?

—From the movie *E.T.*

VALUE CHAINS

In the movie *E.T.*, the extraterrestrial wants to call home telepathically. Had he been born on this planet, he might have tried the old children's game of communicating over a distance by talking into two tin cans connected by a string pulled tight. We have come a long way from the chatter, the string, and the cans, yet they are useful as concepts to describe the three essential links in the economic value chains in business and in education, and to understand how these value chains are changing.

The economic value chain in business begins with suppliers who provide raw materials, then passes to the manufacturers of the product or service, then to distributors, and finally to those who deliver the product or service to the customer. Value chains in industrial and information economies are made up of the same links, but, typically, there is a difference in the way these links are combined:

Typical Industrial Economy Value Chain

Supply ➡ Manufacture ➡ Distribution/ ➡ Customer
Delivery

Typical Information Economy Value Chain

Supply/ ➡ Distribution ➡ Delivery ➡ Customer
Manufacture

Distribution and delivery were generally treated as a single activity in the value chain of the industrial economy, but with the major importance of telecommunications in the information economy, distribution and delivery are very different activities, both of which add value to a product or service. For example, cable companies distribute shows, and your television delivers them. At the same time, the information economy makes less of a distinction between the supplier and manufacturer than did the industrial economy. Desktop publishing, for example, enables an author to be both supplier and manufacturer. In essence, then, there are three major links in today's economic value chain: the chatter, the string, and the can. Those who create and manufacture the offerings are the chatter, those who distribute them are the strings, and those who deliver them to customers are the can.

Although we usually don't think of education this way, it also has a chain that consists of the same three links. Suppliers upstream provide the chatter by creating data, information, and knowledge resources used to educate. These include the books, software, television programs, and other resources people use to learn. Microsoft, McGraw-Hill, and Metro-Media, for example, "manufacture" chatter. In today's economy the manufacture of information is often of more economic value than the manufacture of industrial goods, and this is why Microsoft is worth more than General Motors.

Chatter is transmitted to customers through a distribution system, the string. Distribution in the industrial economy usually involved some sort of transportation, which added little of economic value to the manufacturer or the customer. In this information economy, however, the string that carries the chatter to the customer is an electronic distribution system. As such, the string is an important link in the economic value chain.

The can is the means by which chatter is delivered to the customer. For students, schools and teachers are cans. For employee learners, the cans are corporate training programs. For consumers, smart products and services are the major delivery mechanisms. Today, computers, phones, televisions, recorders, and faxes, singly and blended together in any number of combinations, are cans typically used at home or home offices and in the workplace.

Although our education system has been a public one for over a century, only the means of delivery, the schools, have been public. The other links in the education value chain have always been for profit. With the development of information technologies, however, private suppliers and distributors farther up the chain are in many ways displacing schools by bringing learning directly to consumers, in this case students. As the explosive growth of the non-school-based education industry continues, the entire economic value chain in education will be transformed.

In the industrial economy, knowledge suppliers, manufacturers, and distributors were always in the private sector, while public education focused exclusively on delivery downstream. Government might decide which textbooks to buy for public school classrooms throughout a state, for example, but the books were written for profit, by private individuals, and were published for profit by private corporations. Many educational activities, therefore, have always been profit-making endeavors, while others that were once ignored now present significant economic opportunities.

For some information- and knowledge-intensive companies, the string operates more like a pipeline. They see education as "throughput" and learning as "output." Shakespeare and physics can flow through as readily as airline reservations and engine maintenance instructions. American Airlines, Arthur Andersen, AT&T, and the Baby Bells all operate such pipelines. Their competence lies in how, not what, they distribute, and they lower unit costs by keeping volume up. Their instructional techniques are designed for a wide variety of customers, including company employees, adult training programs, and schools.

To grow fast, a training company has to be highly leveraged. One way to do this is for its instructional materials and techniques to be driven by computers, telephones, and TVs, more than by teachers, even though good teachers will always be needed. In the industrial economy, by contrast, media-based learning consisted of little more than books and blackboards. Today multimedia learning is an important component of the education systems being built by business. Tomorrow it may be the major component.

The largest an instructor-led training company can grow is to about $20 million, and infrastructure costs begin to erode profit margins at around $12 million. Public schools run into this problem when a large portion of their budgets are tied up in plant and infrastructure, including layers of management. Media-based models of learning, by contrast, offer 60–70 percent margins. They operate on the same financial curve as software, where the first unit is very expensive and the nth is cheap.

The product mix of business-led education will favor technology more than teachers because media are so highly leveraged. One good instructor outfitted with ten intelligent computers can outpace ten mediocre teachers with unlimited textbooks. As long as teachers unions and public education systems continue to resist this reality, they will continue to decline.

The relative importance of the individual businesses that provide the chatter, the string, and the can is shifting. As these three links in the education chain integrate and merge, they are creating unified, almost seamless networks of megaindustries. Information technology in the travel industry today, for example, ties together airlines, hotels, car rentals, cruise lines, railroads, ferries, travel agencies, tour wholesalers, travel insurance companies, and even bon voyage merchandisers. The transportation industry is likewise integrating air, sea, and land transport into a unified global system.

In the industrial sector, each sale to the final customer is registered electronically along every point in the chain. Shipping knows to reorder, manufacturing knows to build another unit, purchasing adds that much more to each part order, and so on. The same thing happens in the restaurant business. Another lettuce is ordered for every x number of salads sold, and wholesalers and farmers factor in the numbers and adjust accordingly. In health care, information technology ties together pharmaceutical companies, doctors, pharmacists, hospitals, hospital suppliers, health insurers, and law offices.

What is happening in these industries will also take place in education. The cans, the delivery terminals and outlets at the end of the education value chain, used to be a near monopoly of government-run schools. Almost everything in the supply, manufacture, and distribution sectors, by contrast, remained in the private sector. Today a great variety of computerized terminals have become major outlets in the delivery of learning and education, and most of them are in the private sector, outside of schools. The more humanized these consumer learning terminals become, the more they chip away at the monopoly over delivery that schools once enjoyed.

EDUCATING WITHOUT SCHOOLS

The joining of computers and communications has only begun, and it has already redefined entire value chains in many industries. As it emerges, the megaindustry created by the union of computers, communications, entertainment, media, and publishing will deliver education and learning in such new ways and vast amounts that it will parallel, rival, and in some instances even displace schools as the major deliverer of learning. Without taking over schools, business is an unwitting competitor to the education establishment.

Although it is a classic development, schools for the most part don't recognize this shift. Like many aging companies, schools are generally slow to perceive external threats and slower still to respond. Ignoring new information technologies, they recognize competitive threats only from a small group of traditional players and discount threats that come from startups and upstarts outside their usual playing field. Public school educators mistakenly define their competition as the not-for-profit private schools, missing the stronger competitor that is bypassing them entirely. Business school educators make the same mistake. Institutions like Stanford and Dartmouth define their competitors as Wharton and Northwestern, but seldom as McDonald's and Motorola universities.

School systems are traveling on a familiar path. IBM stayed locked into mainframes and moved into PCs very late. General Motors stayed with big cars and missed the threat from small foreign cars. Sears thought it had a lock as the nation's retailer and ignored the threat from discounters like Wal-Mart. In the same way, the public school system thinks of itself as America's educator and is still inclined to look down upon business as an unworthy competitor. This is a tragic and unnecessary mistake, because—unlike the PC makers, the foreign auto makers, and the discounters—business doesn't even want to take over the schools.

Meanwhile students are nowhere as hesitant as their schools. They have taken to new educational technologies in droves, but as customers, outside of school. Young kids hooked on Nintendo and sophisticated computer learning games may make no distinction between learning play at home and educational work at school. Older kids have their CD players, boom boxes, camcorders, beepers, and PCs. They, too, will not wait for their schools to catch up. Without intending or realizing it, by using information technology, by humanizing it and advancing it to knowledge-based smart products, business is coming to displace school as the locus of learning.

In all these cases—computers, cars, retailing, public school education—the declining institution has focused on how to improve its internal operations, while the major threat came externally in a form that was not recognized. All parties use the new technology. But the defenders, looking internally and backward, have used it to become more efficient at their declining activity. They try to automate the past. The newcomers, on the other hand, use the new technologies to redefine their activity, restructuring the industry itself.

In education, part of this redefinition is a new sense of the value chain. Information technologies become involved in delivering education directly, on network strings and through computer cans, without going through schools. Adobe's first seminar on electronic photography, for example, bypassed colleges, drew four hundred participants, and grossed a quarter of a million dollars in tuition. Schools are also being displaced by suppliers such as publishing and entertainment industries and by distributors such as phone and cable companies. Information technologies are integrating value chains, displacing links that aren't contributing adequately, and causing players all along the chain to access the customer directly.

This same redefinition can be seen in health care, where self-administered, over-the-counter tests are increasingly displacing the more costly variety performed by physicians. Diabetes blood sugar tests, for example, used to be done in hospitals and took twenty-four hours for the results. Now they can be done in your bathroom at home and take half a minute. A do-it-yourself HIV test, with instant results, is currently in development. Traditionally, the medical community has resisted such tests, claiming they are unreliable. The public, however, sees the overwhelming advantage in time, cost, and freedom from control by an intermediating professional.

However, what hospitals come to realize, only after they have lost a niche to a self-administered home-testing product, is that they have been freed from low-order functions and are better able to focus on more value-added activities. Schools, too, should view the self-administered home- and personal-learning technologies in the same light. If history is a predictor, this probably won't happen for one to two more decades. Schools are one generation, and a technology platform, behind business.

In the business of health care, individual doctors and hospitals are now being integrated into HMOs. Will we see a similar integration of teachers, schools, and business into LMOs (learning maintenance organizations) in education? To a great degree this is what we call community colleges. Like HMOs, they too are growing rapidly.

HUMANIZING, THE NEXT TECHNOLOGY PLATFORM

Major economic shifts require new technology platforms. The shifts in learning, first to data, then to information, and now to knowledge, required technological advances to achieve each subsequent step. The CPU, or central processing unit, was the new technology that got us started with data and the computer age. When the focus shifted from just processing data to sharing and communicating them, the ability to integrate computers and communications in networks became the next great technology platform. This made it possible to informationalize businesses.

The advance from information to knowledge will require yet another new technology platform. It will reside in our ability to integrate and use all the existing technologies as easily as we now use the phone and TV. This time around, the focus will be on "humanizing" information technologies so that they become more natural, more versatile, and more responsive to the needs of the individual customer.

Some rather stunning advances in this direction are already under way, in fact, all of which play important roles in humanizing information technology so that we can learn how to put it to productive use, as knowledge.

Voice Recognition

Of all of the pieces necessary to humanize technology, the most important is voice recognition, or what might more colloquially be called "chip chat." The purpose of voice recognition is to enable people to talk to—and ultimately with—computers, tele-visions, and all the other electronic technologies in our lives, rather than having to use keyboards and complex codes or pro-cedures to communicate with them. In this way they become a medium for communication rather than a tool.

The technology that recognizes the spoken word already exists in very elementary form, and you've probably heard it. If your child has called you on the phone "collect," you know that the operator is a voice, programmed to ask you, "Say 'yes' if you accept the charge." A "yes" response is recognized, the call is put through, and you are charged. A "no" is also recognized, and the call is cut off. When you try to fudge it and say, "Hey, wait a minute," you get nothing but a repeat of the original message.

Bellcore, the research arm of the seven regional Bell phone companies, has developed a system that converts demisyllables of speech (the syllable is split in the middle of the vowel) from an analog to a digital signal, and the system is being refined to understand a variety of accents, pronunciations, and voices. When operational, within a few years, it will be used to answer live directory assistance calls (411), which could cut costs by millions of dollars.

Machine-synthesized voices, in lieu of human operators, are the corollary of voice recognition. Today they are getting good enough so that we can't always tell the difference between a person and a machine. Combining voice recognition with Orator, Bellcore's text-to-voice synthesizer, could result in phone com-pany services that "read and speak" electronic mail messages, announce who is calling before the phone is picked up, and match names and addresses to phone numbers.

Another common example of voice recognition is devices that first entered the market in 1992 to program your VCR by speak-ing the information into it in response to prompts. The next stage will be to store the programs digitally, so that you can arrange them at will and retrieve them by asking "Please show me what programs I've got in the sports file, the movie file, and the cook-ing file." We can expect our files to have voice annotations, syn-opses, or personal commentary that we can record along with them. Also, if we missed recording a program when it was broad-cast, we will be able to order it up—again, of course, in plain spoken language—from a central storage system run by our local television station, cable company, home video store, or retrieval service.

Voice recognition, like many new technologies, is almost here, although each seemingly simple step toward this "humanized" technology is frustratingly difficult to accomplish. Early applica-tions will replace push buttons with voice. You'd like to be able to activate your car phone, for example, simply by speaking rather than by pushing buttons. And you would rather say, "Call home" than "Call 376-4275." Voiceprints are as individual as finger-prints. Other applications, therefore, will be for security, using voiceprints to access bank accounts and home security alarms.

Voice recognition is still in the early stages of development. It appeals to early adopters, bless their technical hearts, who will work out the bugs for the rest of us, probably spending more time trying to make it happen than most of us feel it is worth. The technology will probably see wide application among business and individual users before the end of the decade, and within two decades its product and service applications will find their way into use in schools.

Touch Technologies

Alan Kay, one of Apple's major research scientists, points out that in the past the human interface with computers was to remember and type. Currently it is to see and point. In the next decade, he says, "gesture and speech" will become the major interface with computers. Touching is an elementary kind of gesture. More so-phisticated gestures will come when video technologies interpret more subtle body language and combine these with voice recog-nition.

The touch screen is already a familiar and humanizing element. At the Hertz car rental agency, you can touch screens to indicate your destination and receive a printout of directions. Some bank ATMs still have keyboards, but soon all will be touch screens to indicate withdrawals or deposits. Some small neighborhood stores have touch screen cash registers that prepare itemized bills. Many restaurants and fast-food chains use them for more coordinated efforts such as order entry, inventory control, and itemized receipts. It will soon be as possible to reach out and touch some screen as it is now to "reach out and touch someone." The screen will react to you as readily as does the person.

In an educational format, touch screens have been used for toddlers to point to objects as an engaging way to play learning games. Despite their relative maturity as a technology, however, touch screens are not yet being used in school environments. Their main benefit has been to find an easier and more natural way to enter responses and other information for people who have no computer training.

An advancement beyond simple touch screens makes use of an infrared beam that traces the movements of your head or hand, enabling a computer to respond to movements or gestures. Such technology is used at the Media Lab at MIT for war games and at Xerox's Palo Alto Research Center for presentations. Both labs are also experimenting with another kind of touch: the ability to sense and feel objects in the new world of virtual reality. Over five thousand people have now "entered" a proposed church building that exists only in an architectural computer program. With special glasses, the viewer can see the new space in three dimensions. New virtual reality games operate the same way. An even newer technology will enable visitors or players actually to touch and feel the objects they can see. That may be getting almost too close to humanizing for comfort.

Handwriting Recognition

Making sense of all the scribbles and scrawls that pass for handwriting, but are recognizable only to the creator's eye, is another feat that will humanize information technology and advance our learning by making powerful tools more accessible to everyone.

Touch screens force you to choose from a menu, but pen systems let you handwrite any manner of inquiries, notes, or instructions. Pen-based technologies are a next step into the future. With a computer pen or stylus, such as comes with the GO system, you can take notes about your meeting, and the software will interpret your handwriting. This is no easy task even for another human. Not to fear, however, because good pen-based software can be instructed to learn what you mean when you scrawl an *m* followed by *e* halfway across the page.

There's a huge market for this technology among nontypers and those who "hunt and peck." The general rule of thumb is that 80 percent of the population cannot type. Also, typing on keyboards is impractical or out of place in many circumstances. If you're at a conference or in an interview, pencil and paper would be natural, but tapping on keys would be inappropriate, and if you're at a concert when an idea strikes, clicking keys would make you persona non grata.

Some handheld communications devices have no keyboards and accept entries either by voice or by handwriting. Mastering handwriting involves pen-based subtechnologies. The pens of many handheld devices already on the market, for example, double as antennas for cellular phone connections. AT&T advertises that you can now send a handwritten fax from the beach.

Handwriting technology is surely one that teachers will appreciate. Perhaps the worst task facing a teacher is that of reading and grading handwritten reports. Since students can use this technology to translate their efforts into text without typing, teachers should be less resistant to its use than they have been to the use of other technological advances. The need to train software to recognize each individual's handwriting, however, will slow up adoptions. Again, individual consumers and business will likely embrace such technology years before students, teachers, and schools.

Video

Videophones that display the speaker's picture on a screen have been around for many years but were unused until recently because the price was too high and the picture unclear or too jumpy. Now several technological advances have trimmed costs considerably; by the end of the decade videophones should be as common as fax machines. Fiber optics, camera miniaturization, and new picture compression techniques were the main technologies that have made video transmission affordable.

TV clips and videophone conversations can be captured and stored on computer terminals. Handheld videocameras are a lot of fun, but using them can be time consuming and tedious. Remember how many slide trays you accumulated in the sixties and seventies? How about video or TV clips that you can edit and store on your computer? Using voice-activated video, you can call up the clips and send them to your family reunion when you can't be there in person.

When you can capture TV and home video on a touch screen at home, or store them on a computer, you are equipped not only to play movies, a feature welcomed by general consumers and especially couch potatoes, but also to make movies, an option of interest to employees and students. Combine this technology with cable or phone lines, and all those video rental stores with their racks of cassettes will be reduced to empty warehouses.

Personal Agents[1]

Agents are people who act for others by their authority. They come in two varieties, general and special. General agents are those whose authority is defined by the character of their business, such as consignees, factors, and shipmasters. Special agents have limited authority, like ticket agents, travel agents, and FBI agents. In today's information technologies, however, agents don't have to be people wrapped in raincoats; they can be computer codes "wrapped" in friendly little objects called *icons,* on a computer screen.

You don't have to know or care about what's wrapped inside an object for it to do its job. The "it," moreover, is not some hard-wired thing, but a set of instructions. In other words, the intelligence is located in the software. Computer visionary Alan Kay captures this distinction neatly when he says that "hardware is nothing more than software that has been prematurely crystallized." Companies like General Magic are working to provide "intelligent agent" software that can be put into a range of products to make them intelligent. In testimony to the anticipated scope of their use, General Magic has entered into partnerships with Apple, AT&T, Matsushita Electric, Motorola, Philips, and Sony.

Programming in early computers was based on lots of rules, and we struggled to understand the technology and make it work. Now we can just turn the key, push the button, click the mouse, speak a command, or touch the screen—and it works. Sharing and communicating with the technology also became easier, and we began to learn from it. With humanization, the technology also learns from us, the ones who use it. Its learning agents are the computer codes, wrapped up in those little objects on the screen that can look like a mailbox, a telephone, a spy in a raincoat, or a smiling face you can give a name to. The more humanized these agents are, the more they promote learning. For now they are the highest end of the knowledge business.

In reality, agents are software programs, related to artificial intelligence and expert systems, that under your tutelage can develop personal profiles of what you customarily do. Do you always throw away junk mail and periodically check prices on the mutual funds you own? Then your agent will do these things for you. An agent is your personal assistant and gets to know you the way good executive assistants get to know their bosses. It can help you pack for a trip by consulting weather forecasts. It can determine the best routes for driving by tapping into map and travel information. It can call a cab while you're sitting nervously at a prolonged business meeting, worrying that you'll miss your flight. It can make a hotel reservation or cancel one you won't need. Combine all this with voice recognition, and you simply speak these requests to your agent on the computer screen.

In the office, agents will handle smart messages, smart envelopes, and smart mailboxes. Smart messages may include buttons that when pressed trigger some response—like the "R" in RSVP. A smart envelope might know that "if Jeri doesn't pick up my e-mail message in the next hour, send it to her via cellular fax." Smart mailboxes might leave most mail at your office but automatically deliver urgent messages to a device called a "personal communicator" or a "personal digital assistant" that you carry in your briefcase. When they become more a part of the humanized landscape, maybe we'll call them something like "Bob."

Motorola predicts that by the turn of the century twenty million workers will be carrying such wireless devices. These mini–learning stations will unintentionally assault schools' lockstep on learning because, with them, people will enter and leave education on a personal, as needed basis—in real time, not semester time. In fact, all of these humanizing technologies will spread learning among consumers and employees long before they will be encouraged for student use. Actually, it wouldn't be at all surprising if students were initially barred from using them, the same way they were prohibited at first from using electronic calculators.

INTERACTIVE MULTIMEDIA

Multimedia will merge all these information technologies (and others). Multimedia integrates all the data types—text, sound, images, and motion pictures—into powerful packages. In the hands of a skilled TV or film producer, multimedia can produce emotion-packed learning sequences that are much more effective than the words and pictures in any textbooks.

Far and away the largest application for multimedia today is in employee training. Federal Express has a multimedia training system to support 35,000 couriers and service agents. It combines TV-quality video with voice, text, and graphics to teach its employees how to interact with customers, meet international requirements, and test their own performance. Holiday Inn has installed a multimedia program to train its 1,600 hotel managers. It takes the dullest subject in the hotel business, rate and inventory management, and turns it into a motivating tool to raise revenue per hotel bed. One manager boosted revenues $10 per room per day. That's a lot of money—about $20,000 per location, or $32 million for the company. The second largest multimedia application is for learning in schools, particularly off-campus or distance learning. IBM, for example, has distance learning projects in association with California Polytechnic, RPI, and the state of Alabama.

Multimedia now commands prizes the way TV films and programs get Emmy Awards. Arnowitz Productions won the multimedia gold medal in the New York International Film Festival in 1991 for its *Living World* program on animals in the St. Louis Zoo. The program allows teachers to choose from four and a half hours of full-motion video segments, two hours of animal sounds, a complete copy of the country's most widely used biology textbook, and five hundred slides about ecology and zoology.

Master teachers and forward-looking educators have hailed interactive multimedia because it transforms the learning process from passive to active. The control shifts to the individual user, the learner, where it should be. When control shifts to the learner, motivation goes up and learning is enhanced.

Television alone does the reverse. It is an electronic technology that is a one-way street: it broadcasts to you. All the power is in the hands of the producer and the network companies that schedule the timing. The viewer is captive, and the motivation is passive. Interactive multimedia is for active users, not passive viewers. Good television is often said to touch the heart but not the brain. Interactive multimedia will strive to touch the heart *and* the brain.

Contrary to the Big Brother image of technology as intimidator, multimedia acts as an initiator to benefit learners. In conventional classroom teaching, some students learn quickly while others take much longer to reach only the average. Tests of multimedia learning, by contrast, show that all participants reach a relatively high level at the same time, and faster than the best participants in conventional learning. The Big Six accounting firm Ernst & Young asked its audit partners to calculate their savings from multimedia desktop learning. Approximately $1 million was saved by decreasing classroom time from two weeks to one, learning was up 15 percent, consistency improved 25 percent, and what used to take 9.0 hours to teach took 3.5 hours to learn.[2] The reason: Multimedia can adjust to different styles of learning and intelligence.

Harvard researcher Howard Gardner revolutionized our understanding of the field by asserting that there are at least seven types of intelligence and learning: linguistic intelligence (a poet's, for example); logical-mathematical intelligence (a scientist's); musical intelligence (a composer's); spatial intelligence (a sculptor's or airplane pilot's); body-kinesthetic intelligence (a dancer's or athlete's); interpersonal intelligence (a salesperson's or teacher's); and intrapersonal intelligence (a philosopher's).

We all have different types of intelligence and learning styles. You can take simple tests now, for example, to determine whether you learn best through auditory (listening to a lecture) or visual (watching a video) cues. Other learners favor analytic (reading a report) or kinesthetic (learning by doing) styles. Teachers who can adjust to these differences are the most effective; as a corollary, teaching through any medium is most effective when it can adapt to different learning styles.

Humanizing information technology promotes learning precisely because it can adopt your preferred style. Take music, for example. You can learn to play the piano from the software programs available when you buy your first electronic keyboard—in far less time and for less money than you would spend on conventional piano lessons. Humanized information technologies are less intimidating. When technology is teacher, you can ask dumb questions that you would probably be afraid to ask a human teacher. One of the maxims used in corporate classrooms is "Make Misstakes, Ask Questions, Cheat, and Have Fun." Humanized information technology is not judgmental. It doesn't make you wear a dunce cap, sit in the corner, or stay after school. It's infinitely patient. Remember giving up in frustration at having to respond when a young child asked "why" so many times? Humanized information technology knows why and doesn't give up until you know it, too.

The ultimate in humanized information technology is virtual reality (VR). We had our first experience with a Sega game battling pterodactyls. Wearing helmet, goggles, and touch-sensitive gloves, we shot down one of the monsters. But just when we thought we were safe, another flew into our three-dimensional space, its talons grabbed us by the scruff of our virtual necks, and suddenly, gripped by fear, our stomachs told us we were flying out of control. To say this was lifelike, or similar to roaring down the Grand Canyon at Cinemax, is to compare a pussycat with a snarling lion. Someone else in the room who had tried it said, "Don't give this to anyone over sixty without a medical doctor present."

The question many people ask when they first experience VR is whether ultimately it will be the most *de*humanizing of technologies. For example, one affronted mother said, "Why not just put one of these helmets on your child in the crib?" And another retorted, "Why even bother to have children when you can have sex with your helmet?" Not everyone is so skeptical. A woman who had just used VR to walk through her yet-to-be-built house was very impressed. She gave the skeptics pause by remarking, "Imagine how many students you could turn on to Shakespeare through VR."

BUSINESS BEFORE SCHOOLS

Business was the first to use computers when they were introduced in the 1950s, long before schools and government. In the four decades since, the business sector has gone through several stages of usage, and these stages predict how this technology will be assimilated and used in education.

The first use was to cut costs and improve internal operating efficiencies. This meant streamlining and automating old tasks, never questioning the tasks themselves. Only two decades later did questions arise as to whether this increased productivity or not, and a decade after that the general consensus was that it had not.

The next stage came with the networking of computers, which connected businesses with their customers and linked players on value chains from beginning to end. This stage began in the late 1970s, and in little over a decade it was apparent that computer networking was transforming the way business was conducted, even redefining businesses and entire industries.

Airlines started by computerizing their reservations systems. Only much later did they develop frequent flyer programs, and in-flight multimedia edutainment looms ahead. Banks first applied computer technology to back-office operations, and direct links with customers through ATMs came with the networking stage, although fifteen years after it was first proposed, home banking has still to reach takeoff. Using computers, consumer goods manufacturers were able to dictate terms to retailers like the supermarket chains. Then, using the computer networking, retailers like Wal-Mart and Toys "Я" Us reversed the leverage of power and now dictate terms to manufacturers. In the future again through computer networking, customers will co-create with retailers the products that manufacturers will be asked to make.

Now entering the fifth decade of computer use, and with the advent of new humanized information technologies, businesses are once again experiencing profound changes. The tools provided by a more humanized infrastructure will enable the businesses that use it to add knowledge to their already information-intensive activities. The use of computer technology by the military followed the same stages. First it automated back-office operations like payroll and purchasing. Only recently has it used information technology to develop smart weapons and thereby revolutionize warfare. Similarly, hospitals first computerized patient lists and billings and only later implemented smart new products and high-tech services like CAT scans and MRIs.

Schools have been among the most laggard institutions in using the information technologies of the computer age. Telephones are everywhere except in classrooms. Educational TV is seen more often at home than in school. By and large, schools are still in the first stage of computer use. Some are networked for attendance, grades, record keeping, and electronic catalogs for libraries, but these automate support operations rather than transform methods of instruction.

It's not that there is no computer technology in schools. While resources per student are small, the base is growing rapidly. As of 1992 there were 2.8 million personal computers in schools. That is 1 computer for every 13 students, a tenfold improvement over the 1 to 125 ratio a decade ago. Quality Education Data (QED) Inc., a market research firm that tracks technology in schools, reports that school use of computer networks grew 64 percent from 1992 to 1993, the use of video disks grew by 45 percent, and the use of CDs grew by 48 percent. Satellite dishes to receive instructional programs also grew by 87 percent in this one year alone.[3]

Thus the numbers are growing, but too often the technology is not used innovatively, if it is used at all. Apple, for example, cites cases of technology acquired but not used.[4] In California, at the Menlo Oaks Middle School, ten secondhand IBM PCs sat stacked and untouched in the middle of the computer lab, next to ten donated, broken and unrepaired Apple Macintosh computers. No one knew how to make use of the equipment.

Some schools do use information technology successfully. Since 1991, the West Ottawa Public School near Holland, Michigan, has linked 5,500 students, teachers, administrators, and parents in a fiber-optic communications network throughout the district. The system, which connects eleven buildings and three hundred classrooms, was put in place to provide easy access to information, resources, and people. Ten-year-olds can produce videos that may be seen in any class or home. For assignments, students can also access sophisticated databases from class, library, computer lab, or home. The system facilitates individualized learning programs, and parents can contact teachers during school hours by classroom telephone to convey important messages and to schedule meetings. Teachers can enter attendance and grades electronically from wherever they are, and administrators can post meetings and memos by electronic mail. Perhaps the only drawback to the system is that the whole district can see students' homework displayed on the cable channel.

This rural, rapidly growing suburban district twenty-five miles southwest of Grand Rapids is not rich. Statewide annual per pupil expenditures are between $2,300 and $9,000, and West Ottawa spends $4,800. The $5.5 million technology project was paid for with a bond issue passed by voters. Unfortunately West Ottawa is an exception to the rule. Parents and voters commonly resist this kind of investment, and teachers resist on grounds that television, telephones, and movies entertain but don't educate. This need no longer be the case.

The experience of one New Mexico high school was more typical. Students in an integrated social studies, English, and science program were asked to present a report on teenage smoking. Videocam interviews with smokers and nonsmokers at the school were integrated with scientific findings and social statistics. Other team projects included reports on rap music, graffiti artists, and "rad" architecture.

This high school program was built to handle a hundred students, and four hundred students were on the waiting list for year two. Nevertheless, the program had difficulty getting funded for a second year, even though it was supported by a major consumer electronics company. Many teachers outside the program felt threatened by the changes it represented. They didn't know how to use the new technologies, how to grade film reports instead of written ones, how to handle the integration of English, science, and social studies, or what role to play when the students controlled their own projects and went off campus in teams on school time.

The students were given camcorders and computers to edit their films, but the school administrators wouldn't give them a telephone line to access multimedia libraries because they were worried about controlling long-distance charges, even though any phone line can be set up for restricted use. It would have required rewiring the school's PBX, and even though moderate costs were involved, the real roadblock was the implied threat to the administration's psyche and power. Although the program has survived, its founders want to remove it from the politicking of the high school and reconstitute it as an independent magnet program, much as business would create a "skunkworks."

The technologies for information age learning remain far more abundant in our homes than in our schools. Virtually all homes have telephones and televisions, three-quarters have VCRs, 60 percent have cable, and 20 percent have camcorders, faxes, compact disc players, and personal computers. Half of the sixty million PCs in the United States are in homes, together with thirty million Nintendo units. Moreover, all these boxes are getting hooked together faster and faster.

In the business world, companies provide a barrage of new technological products and services, and their customers learn how to use them. In the school world, however, the process is reversed: the consumers are in the lead. Students, as consumers, are using, and learning from, the new technologies before their parents and teachers. Only when this generation of student-learners is itself old enough to become parents and teachers will information technology finally pervade the school world.

In sum, schools are a technological generation behind in their use of computers and information technology. Businesses have to use the new technologies or they don't survive. Schools do not. They can and have resisted their use for decades. The results are inevitable. First, schools are losing out to those institutions that do adopt learning technologies. Education stays in schools and falters, while learning migrates to consumers and employees in the marketplace and thrives. Second, with the advent of humanized information technologies, which are being quickly adopted by businesses, consumers, and employees, the gap will widen, and it will take schools longer, perhaps even decades, to catch up.

This is a pity. Ideally, business and education should work together, but declining institutions seldom reinvigorate themselves with new technologies, and schools are no exception. The problem is a political and human issue more than a technological one. Ironically, learning technologies will revolutionize business before they revolutionize schools.

CHAPTER 4

L'EARNING POWER

What one knows is, in youth, of little moment;
they know enough who know how to learn.

—HENRY ADAMS

WORLDS APART

A university professor and a corporate trainer sat next to each other on a commuter train. The professor had just given several lectures to students of art history; the corporate trainer had just completed a grueling day of leadership training for corporate executives. The professor was curious about his seatmate's profession and was somewhat taken aback when she told him that she was an educator in a "university" larger than his. He wore a tweed jacket and carried a briefcase bulging with papers; she was in jeans and carried a notebook computer. He was tenured and earned a comfortable living; she had survived the last company reorganization and was paid double his salary.

"What do you teach?" he asked.

"I don't teach," she replied. "I organize learning." Put off his guard, he asked, "What subjects?"

"Managerial values and behaviors for the next decade," she said. "And you?"

"Modern art of the past century."

Raising her computer, she asked, "Do you use these things?"

"No," he said, "I'm in the humanities department."

"Me too," she said. "But they call it the human resources department."

Like ships passing in the night, these two educators couldn't seem to connect. Both are engaged in teaching and learning, but their methods, their goals, and their purposes are different. He's teaching lessons from the past, she's teaching trends for the future. He's comfortable with the lecture technique, she uses computer technology networks. He would say that the arts are essential to a society's values, she would reply that challenging managerial values and behavior is her day-to-day job. One practices teaching, the other promotes learning. Both refer to themselves as educators.

In *The Reckoning,* David Halberstam writes about how General Motors executives in the early 1970s dismissed Japanese cars because they were small, exclusively front-wheel drive, and painted white. This is a familiar reaction. When confronted with something new that does not fit into prior classifications in our head, we deny its existence, dismiss its importance, or project the problem it represents onto someone else. When face to face with employee education or corporate universities, traditional educators do the same thing. They ignore its existence or diminish its importance. In doing so, they miss four critical points about employee education:

- First, employee education is the fastest-growing learning segment in our society and involves a lot more than just training.
- Second, employee education focuses on learning for managers and professionals, productivity for service workers, and basic schooling for unskilled workers, in that order.
- Third, in its use of learning technologies, customer and employee education provided by business is more revolutionary than the education provided by business schools.

- Fourth, employee education foreshadows changes in other education market segments.

Saturn Corporation is a good example of the trends in employee education. This $3 billion startup by General Motors was launched in Tennessee to build an American car to compete with the Japanese. To succeed, GM executives felt that they had to build a new factory that incorporated the latest car-manufacturing technology and employed a new and highly skilled and motivated workforce that practiced the latest wisdom about behavior and learning. Each management and union employee spends over one hundred hours per year in training, making Saturn one of the most education-intensive corporations.

Even more important than the number of hours spent in training is the fact that Saturn is using learning to revolutionize the business. Learning permeates the entire organization, including relations between union and management and between manufacturers and dealers. Decision making is done jointly and cooperatively. Customer relations are radically different. Satisfied customers, for example, make up half of the "staff" for Saturn booths at auto shows, exhibiting a cultlike loyalty similar to the loyalty of Apple customers.

Saturn employees start their formal training on "Excel," an experiential course. First, they go through a "blind trust walk," where one person is blindfolded and led by a teammate through an obstacle course. Second, they climb a forty-foot-high wall, working together in teams of three. Third, they return to a class setting to discuss issues of "truth, accountability, support, trust, and empowerment." A set of individual and corporate values develops from these experiences, including a dedication to teamwork, a commitment to excel, trust and respect for the individual, acknowledgment of the necessity for continuous improvement, and a commitment to build customer enthusiasm.

If this were a traditional school, its graduates would rate a top grade. But this is business, and grading is done differently. Measurable benefits are tied to results in the business, not to performance in the courses. These include the highest sales per outlet in the industry for the six-month period after training, top ratings in the North American Dealer Association's Attitude Survey, and industry leadership in customer enthusiasm and in low sales "consultants" turnover.

Saturn's training program proved so successful that an average of ten companies a day called to ask about its availability. As a result, the company spun it off as Saturn Outside Services (SOS) to provide training to noncompetitive companies for profit. SOS sells leadership and partnership training courses to other companies that want to bring the Saturn experience to their employees. Honeywell, early on, sent its top management team through the Saturn Excel course. This sensible practice is common in business, but not in academic settings. It would be as if the University of Tennessee cloned itself to deliver its best course to the University of Minnesota. In conventional school systems, it is unheard of to send students from one school to another that offers a better course. Sharing is done more to spread cost burdens and broaden offerings than to spread excellence. Despite its scant profits and occasional interdivisional feuding, Saturn is now spreading its lifelong learning techniques to other parts of General Motors. Oldsmobile, Chevrolet, and GM Europe are all "Saturnizing" their operations.

NUMMI (New United Motor Manufacturing, Inc.) is another General Motors Company that has used lifelong learning for ten years now and, with the same 1,800 workers, transformed GM's most unproductive auto factory to its most productive. NUMMI is a strategic alliance, utilizing GM's Freemont, California, plant and Japanese management to produce the GEO Prism. Emphasizing built-in quality, continuous improvement, and teamwork, NUMMI builds a car in twenty-two hours compared with thirty-five to fifty hours in GM's Detroit plants. Also, absenteeism dropped from 24 to 3 percent, and employee satisfaction increased from 65 to 90 percent in seven years.

Thirteen New Harvards

The experience at Saturn is not unique. At a time when conventional K–college segments are shrinking, employees have become the fastest-growing market for learning. Members of the baby boom generation have left schools and campuses and are now in the workplace to continue their learning, which is more work related and conducted by business rather than by schools.

The number of corporate employees receiving formal, budgeted training in 1992 grew by nearly four million people. On average, each of these people had 31.5 classroom contact hours annually, an increase of 126 million additional hours of employee learning in just that one year.[1] If this kind of growth occurred in higher education, it would be the equivalent of almost a quarter million additional full-time college students. To house this many new learners on a college campus, thirteen new universities the size of Harvard would have to be built to handle a single year's growth in corporate education. That is more growth in just one year than enrollment growth in all the new conventional college campuses built in the United States in the thirty years from 1960 to 1990.

By contrast, the president of the University of California scuttled plans to build a tenth campus in 1993, saying that the university was hard-pressed to pay for existing schools. At the same time, and for the first time ever, California showed a net outflow of population due to loss of jobs. The last full-fledged academic universities to be built in the United States were the University of California Davis campus in 1965, the State University of New York (SUNY) campus at Purchase in 1967, and the University of the District of Columbia in 1976. All of the four-year general academic, specialized, and religious universities built between 1970 and 1990 would have handled just over 1 percent of the new entrants in corporate education in the single year of 1992. Employee education is not growing 100 percent faster than academia, but 100 times—or 10,000 percent—faster.

This remarkable growth in employee education often goes unnoticed because it is submerged in the workforce, takes place part-time, and is not very glamorous. Yet the numbers will only increase. One reason for the surge is demographic: members of the baby boom generation, now in their thirties and forties, are in their most productive work years. Another reason is that employers must often undertake remedial training of workers ill prepared by their public education. Yet according to *Training* magazine, the bulk of training goes to middle and upper management. Only about 10 percent of funds for employee training goes to workers.

The most important reason for the growth in employee education is the rapid pace of technological change and the increased importance of knowledgeable managers and workers to keep up with these changes. Businesses now have to reeducate their employees throughout their working lives so that they can stay competitive. The occupational half-life—that is, the span of time it takes for one-half of workers' skills to become obsolete—has declined from seven to fourteen years to three to five years, according to the National Research Council.[2]

This is particularly true in engineering. In their first five years working, half of what engineering students learned in college becomes obsolete. Ten years out, less than a quarter of that material is still applicable. In fact, corporate educators have discovered that a real challenge is how to *unlearn* much of this useless obsolete information. One week of training per year is more than most engineers and professionals get. Yet this is not nearly enough just to keep up. That is why a common belief among education-oriented executives is that learning faster and better may be the only sustainable competitive advantage.

A mechanic who understood five hundred pages of repair manuals as recently as 1965 could fix just about any car on the road. Today that same mechanic would need nearly five hundred thousand pages of manuals, equivalent to fifty New York City telephone books.[3] On such a steep curve, employees must be engaged in learning the new material in their field on a regular basis.

Attending courses to brush up is not enough. This can mean an enormous amount of time spent away from the job and is probably unrealistic. What is more logical is that this large dose of training will indeed go on but will become integrated more directly into the fabric of the job itself. It also means that training will focus more on learning than on education—that is, on jumping employees from information to its personal and productive use as knowledge. Slowly, learning will become endemic to the workplace, native not naturalized.

A good rule of thumb is this: The faster a business changes, the more it needs to invest in learning. The shorter the half-life of knowledge, the closer the link has to be between the centers of education and the centers of enterprise. Businesses are responding to this new imperative more rapidly than business schools.

BUSINESS SCHOOLS HARDLY CHANGE

The MBA program in business schools has been an established brand for many years. Most business schools want to extend its life cycle rather than supersede it with a fundamentally new program. To be sure, there have been some second- and third-generation product extensions, such as evening and one-day-per-week programs for those who work, and some business schools have even taken a few of their courses to suburban campuses to attract people as they drive home from work. Some schools offer team teaching and team learning; others beef up their international fare. Course materials have been upgraded, and some class offerings have changed, but the 1960s product is still quite recognizable and serviceable in the 1990s.

The major new direction taken during these past decades has been in executive education, with a panoply of short offerings and an executive MBA. Otherwise not much has changed. Students still come to classes to learn, the classes are still sixty, seventy-five, or ninety minutes long, and courses are still offered in semesters, trimesters, or quarters. Instructors still stand in front of the room and students sit in rows that, at most, have been bent from straight lines into a horseshoe shape for case discussions. Typical classroom technology is still hardly beyond what it was three and four decades ago. Computers are used extensively, but so are pencils. Indeed, the process and products of business school education have changed as little as the process and products of any kind of school education, whereas business itself has gone through revolutions.

Education has not embraced the revolution in information technology the way that business has, and business schools in this regard are clearly more like education than like business. Managers can come to an executive program from anywhere in the world, for example, but the program will not go to them, electronically, wherever they are; learners still have to sit in the same room to hear the lecture. Why can't the best faculty in the best schools deliver courses to employees in any companies that sign up and download them into on-site electronic classrooms? This is not about technology-based education, but about changing mindsets; the technology is an enabler, not the be-all and end-all.

The Harvard Business School, for example, tried and failed to put together all of its informationalized activities. About 30 percent of its revenues comes from the MBA program and another 30 percent from executive programs. Yet, using an academic model rather than a business one, it reached the upper limits of growth in both. These programs are run as maintenance activities; the focus is on sustaining quality rather than expanding. It shows. The MBA program is "very mature," and executive programs are hurting badly. Enrollment in the 1993 Advanced Management Program dropped from 160 to 107, and the middle management program plummeted with 140 slots and only 79 takers. Harvard's executive programs ranked fifteenth out of fifteen in a 1993 *Wall Street Journal* poll. The idea for a one-year MBA program option was an attempt to raise new monies without cannibalizing the school's other offerings. It was rejected.

The other 40 percent of the school's revenues come from information spin-offs. These include the *Harvard Business Review,* the Case Clearing House, the HBS Press, and videotapes. The idea was to take them off campus, put them together as a growth group, and have them lead the way into an electronic future. Three years and several management upheavals later, the program is just getting out of the starting block. Their International Tele-seminar Broadcast, using satellite transmission to alumni clubs worldwide, is a promising beginning.

Businesses are asking management schools to make significant changes in the way they operate. They want their learning customized to specific company and industry needs rather than generic cases. They want programs delivered at their own sites rather than on a distant campus. And they want learning delivered according to their own time schedules rather than in semesters.

An admirable exception to the general tendency is the early exploration by MIT to deliver distance learning by satellite to China. Because of the vast population and great distances, the only way for an American institution to make a contribution of consequence would be to use new telecommunications technologies as the distribution system.

Some corporations are turning to training companies to answer these same needs. DuPont, for example, chose to contract all of its training and development to the Forum Corporation. DuPont spends between $300 million and $500 million per year on training of all sorts. Corporate executives felt they were spending too much money, that quality was variable and there was lots of duplication and no way of measuring impact. They also believed that training was not a core competence for them and that they should contract it to a global player for whom it was.

To lower its costs, DuPont moved training from a fixed to a variable cost so that training budgets became allocated to individual business units and weren't carried as corporate overhead. To raise quality, it repositioned training from a developmental tool for individuals to a strategic tool for the entire business and organization. "The long-term vision," says Gerald Jones, who is running the project for Forum, "is that learning can create competitive advantage."

DuPont chooses to see what it has done as "insourcing" rather than outsourcing because in the first year Forum hired about twenty DuPont trainers, whose salaries are only gradually being phased over to Forum's payroll. In addition to working with DuPont employees, they will train suppliers, customers, and new hires. They will also work with community colleges to provide basic reading and writing skills and operator mechanics training.

The Center for Creative Leadership in Greensboro, North Carolina, is one of the most respected and successful non-business-school leadership development programs in the country. Goodyear alone has sent as many as ten thousand managers over a ten-year period. The sessions typically meet for an intensive week, twice a year for two years. While Goodyear is CCL's largest client, nearly every private and public firm of Fortune 500 size has sent some managers to CCL. No business school can yet boast of such a track record.

The harder the business schools resist their clients' demands, the less they will share in the growth of employee education. Business will create its own systems for developing its managers rather than relying on MBAs perceived as arrogant and inexperienced. Thus, when it comes to education, business is eclipsing the business schools.

EDUCATION-INTENSIVE COMPANIES

The training that does go on in companies is most prevalent in large corporations, especially those that see themselves with knowledge workers, or in education or consulting businesses. Arthur Andersen, for example, the $5 billion accounting and consulting firm, currently spends more than $300 million per year on training. That is 6.5 percent of the firm's 1992 revenues.

Andersen runs an education system comparable in budget to the University of Virginia's and larger than the budgets of Purdue University, Syracuse University, or the University of South Carolina. The major difference is that Andersen's education division is run *by* a business, *for* a business, and it's one of the biggest *in* the business. It operates campuses in Australia, Mexico, Spain, the Netherlands, and the United States, which together serve students from every continent save Antarctica.

The main facility in St. Charles, near Chicago, is a 150-acre campus that was bought from Saint Dominic College in 1971 and transformed into a technology-intensive investment costing over $140 million. It teaches 62,000 professional employees a year, over 35,000 of whom work directly for Andersen. The hefty remainder are clients and outside customers.

Each one of Andersen's auditors, tax advisers, and management consultants spends 130 contact hours in training per year, which amounts to 6.5 percent of their professional time. This is equivalent to half a semester for a traditional college-age student, which also means that Andersen can teach in two weeks what takes a college two months. Employees study more hours daily than do students at nearby Northwestern University. Additionally, every four to five years each professional goes through a major retraining plan. Lifelong learning is practiced, not preached. Even when graduates leave the company, they are always welcomed back as alumni.

Participants have access to golf, lighted tennis courts, a five-lane swimming pool, and cross-country skiing in winter, all on campus. While there is no football stadium, there are three separate lounges for socializing, including a disco for dancing. Over half of Andersen's young consultants, but only 10 percent of the partners, are female. The mayor of St. Charles prefers the Arthur Andersen campus to a traditional one, he says, because "we get all the benefits of a university like Northwestern, except this one also pays taxes."

The campus has a large educational support system. Plane reservations, for example, require ten full-time on-campus travel agents. The campus is the most frequent destination from O'Hare Airport, with 10,400 limousine trips outnumbering the taxis and buses ten to one. There are over 100 classrooms, 1,682 dormitory beds in monklike rooms, and seating for almost 1,000 in various dining rooms. They brew 65,000 gallons of coffee per year, for an average of about a gallon an accountant, and they recycle all the coffee grinds around the many trees and shrubs, which are healthy and politically correct.

Motorola, the $13 billion technology giant, is another big spender on education. In 1980 the company spent $7 million on training and wondered whether it was an excessive sum. Motorola University now spends more than $120 million, 3.6 percent of payroll, and it is considered another leader in corporate learning. Since the company won the coveted Baldrige Award, the company's executives think it is money well invested.

Its educational efforts in China are a case in point. Annual demand for pagers in China zoomed from one million in 1991 to four million in 1993, and Motorola sells its entire Chinese output in the home market. With such enormous future growth in mind, Motorola is laying the groundwork for what may be one of China's largest manufacturing ventures. Although China has hundreds of thousands of engineers, most of those in their mid-thirties and -forties lack the training to adapt to a modern high-tech plant because higher education was devastated by the Cultural Revolution from 1966 to 1976. "Their knowledge of basic science is very strong," says Ko Ching-wen, Motorola's personnel director in Tianjin, "but they don't know how to apply it."

The company is providing hundreds of scholarships to students and faculty in eight universities and donating computer equipment and staff so that schools can set up chip-design labs. It also plans to offer working internships to college students and dispatch managers to Chinese high schools to explain uses of technology. The company is spending millions on in-house training programs, preparing for the startup of its design centers for integrated circuits and telecommunications products in China. Motorola has a career management track called "Cadres 2000" for Chinese executives who will eventually head the Tianjin complex, and it plans to put up to twenty recruits yearly into leadership training programs and rotate them through their operations worldwide.

After forty years as a hardware company, Motorola is repositioning itself to derive 75 percent of revenue from software. "We're shifting from guys who wear plastic pen protectors in their shirt pockets to guys who sport earrings," says a Motorola vice president. Teaching methods reflect similar shifts. Instead of lectures and textbooks, workers and managers learn by "reinventing the work processes" they use. They build mock-ups of their products and design new ways these models could be produced. The company calculates that for every $1 spent on training, it gets $30 in productivity gains over three years. Sales per employee have doubled and profits increased by nearly 50 percent between 1988 and 1993. These achievements have become a "gold standard" for other corporate universities.

Federal Express has gotten high returns from its investments in learning. The company invested nearly $70 million to build a completely automated educational certification system. It spends 4.5 percent of payroll and makes the widest-possible use of interactive videodiscs (IVD) to enhance learning among its forty thousand couriers and customer service agents. There are 1,225 IVD units in seven hundred locations, each with a twenty-five-videodisc (equivalent to 37,500 floppy disks) curriculum that is updated monthly. With IVD, employees get four hours of company-paid study and preparation time and two hours of self-administered tests every six months, for periodic skill upgrades.

The strategy is to "train for knowledge, test for competency, perform to standards, and retrain for recurrent knowledge."[4] The "pay-for-performance/pay-for-knowledge system," begun in 1987, guarantees that all employees "operate from the same book," so that customers get accurate and consistent information. In 1990 Federal Express was the first service company to win the Malcolm Baldrige National Quality Award. The job-knowledge test scores count for 12 percent of each Federal Express employee's six-month performance review.

High growth, retrenching, and rebirthing giants are all increasing their training. At Corning, Inc., by devoting a day per week over two years, workers' pay can rise 20 percent once they certify a new core competency. Microsoft focuses its training on technical support staff, such as software engineers and implementation consultants. The company is training 250 people per week to add to its base of over 2,000 technicians. In its heyday in 1990, IBM's director of education had a budget that exceeded $1 billion. Before its fall the company engaged 7,000 full-time instructors and staff who conducted educational events for more than 18,000 employees on any given day. This should also serve as a warning that education alone cannot rescue a company and can be just as bureaucratic as the rest of the organization.

GM's Chevrolet, which for years did very little training, now focuses on learning as a key strategy in its hoped-for turnaround. Ford advertises that it invests $20 million each month in employee education. If the education arms of GE, AT&T, or IBM were spun off as public universities, their revenues would exceed the budgets of Big Ten powerhouses like Ohio State, Michigan, and Purdue.

"CORPORATE UNIVERSITY" EQUIVALENTS

Corporations will continue to need traditional universities to carry out basic education and research. Nevertheless they will increasingly take on teaching themselves. The formal education that goes on at companies like Arthur Andersen and Motorola is comparable to treatment of similar subjects at top-tier academic institutions. Of course, not all corporate training is that sophisticated, but there has been a boom in the number of "corporate universities" during the past decade. Many of them are simply rechristened training centers, and it is easy to laugh at the notion that they are true universities. But even when they are not, the popularity of the term *university* in a corporate setting speaks to important truths.

The efforts may be meager, but the message is clear: Learning is important, and the intent is grand. It adds prestige to an activity that never before received much attention. It says to the participants, We will teach you what you have to know, at the highest levels, to do your job well and to succeed. When typing pools were first renamed "word-processing centers" a quarter century ago, folks laughed then, too. When "personnel" became "human resources," many thought it was just a cosmetic change for prestige. But such name changes signaled shifts in what had become important.

No matter what the business, companies are creating corporate universities or their equivalents. One of the best known is McDonald's Hamburger University, which concentrates on preparing and serving food. Its campus, also near Chicago, has five dormitories, several ponds on its wooded grounds, and class facilities for simultaneous translation in eighteen languages. When the first McDonald's outlets appeared in Budapest and then Moscow, they had waiting times of an hour or more before you could get a hamburger, leading to jokes about the Russian redefinition of fast food. For many months the Hamburger U campus was flooded with Russians and other Eastern European nationalities who came to learn customer service, a concept previously unheard of.

The Hart Schaffner & Marx University, known as "Suits-U," concentrates on sales training. AT&T's University of Sales Excellence, formerly based in Cincinnati and in Denver, is being decentralized to focus on training for the sales and service of the company's new technology-based products. Now the question for AT&T is how soon it will extend its training to other countries, which over time will constitute a projected 50 percent of its growth.

Not all the expansion of corporate universities is in brick and mortar. The Holiday Inn University campus, for example, was established near Memphis, Tennessee, in 1972. It closed in 1990 and was replaced with a mobile system known as the Road Scholars program. This initiative was composed of sixteen teams of two trainers. Each team was equipped with a customized van, laptop computers, and all the necessary training materials to conduct on-site hotel training as they crisscrossed the United States.

Holiday Inn Worldwide's fastest-growing education needs are in China, where thirty new hotels were opened in 1991 alone. Because the Chinese demanded something to demonstrate their respect for higher education, the company has reinstituted a brick-and-mortar Holiday Inn University there.

The Holiday Inn education challenge is mind-boggling. Imagine a typical hotel manager in the Washington, D.C., area, who was brought up Catholic, graduated from Catholic University of America, and goes to mass every Sunday. He has never traveled outside the United States. His hotel staff of twenty includes three Buddhists from Korea, several Copts from Ethiopia, and a sprinkling of Muslims from Indonesia and Jordan. Those whose religious beliefs he comprehends speak only Spanish, which he has never had time to learn. Even if he had, service employees turn over at an average of a new person every three months, which may mean a new language and a new religion. The average education level of hotel staff is the sixth grade.

In 1993 Holiday Inn Worldwide launched Project Darwin, the largest training initiative in its forty-year history. Project Darwin (so named because it evolves and adapts as the needs change) started in the Americas Division: United States, Canada, Mexico, Latin America, and the Caribbean. There are thirty-three areas, each headed by an area service delivery consultant (ASDC) who lives in the region. ASDCs consult with thirty to thirty-five hotels to improve revenue and service.

Technology plays a critical role in Project Darwin's success. Over fifty trainers and consultants are networked with state-of-the-art laptop and personal computers that access the Holiday Inn Business Intelligence System (BIS). When ASDCs prepare for an on-site consultation, they use the BIS for hotel-specific information and analysis to coach the hotel management. The company has also committed to providing dedicated multimedia training at each of its 1,500 Americas hotels. This "just in time" learning offers the benefits of consistent hotel operations and reduced costs. With its multimedia training initiative, Holiday Inn has become the first multimedia hotel company and one of the largest corporate multimedia users. Holiday Inn Worldwide invests more than double its nearest competitors (Ramada, Marriott, and Hilton) and nearly five times Sheraton in training hours per hotel per year.

How has it all paid off? Customer complaints dropped in some hotels from an average of two hundred a month to only two or three per month. Revenue per room at some hotels increased by as much as 15 percent. Training time for management staff has been condensed from four weeks at the old Holiday Inn University to only five days with Project Darwin. Holiday Inn provides its franchises and their hotels with the training they want, when they want it, and more cost effectively than ever before.

The bottleneck for Holiday Inn is neither money nor training techniques. It's much bigger than that. General managers aren't as sensitive to cultural diversity as they should be. "They need to learn to adapt to radically different beliefs and value systems," said the president of the Americas Division. "Multimedia can teach them rate and inventory, but diversity and turnover in the hospitality industry will always provide a challenge."

Many companies that face similar learning challenges have launched corporate initiatives to meet them. The sheer number and diversity is staggering. Corporate universities include, among many others, the Aetna Institute for Education, American Express Quality University, Apple University, Cigna, Disney University, Dow Chemical's Midland Learning Center, Eastman Kodak, First of America Bank's Quality Service University, General Electric's Management Development Institute, General Motors, GTE, IBM, Intel, the Johnson Controls Training Institute, MasterCard University, Merrill Lynch, Motorola University, Nationwide Insurance, New England Telephone, Pitney-Bowes's and Marriott Hotels' jointly owned Aberdeen Woods Conference Center, Procter & Gamble College, Bristol-Myers Squibb, Sun Oil, 3-M, United Auto Workers/Chrysler National Training Center, and Xerox Document University.

Many traditional academics disdain these corporate "universities." Calling them universities, they feel, cheapens the meaning of the term because they do not have academia's traditions or breadth in either research or teaching. Few of them focus on philosophy and higher truths, but then neither are there many philosophy majors in the traditional colleges. While corporate universities are different, they are not devoid of learning. What they can claim is relevance to the occupational needs of those attending.

The learning that goes on at corporate universities keeps employees valuable to the company and to the marketplace. In an earlier era they would have been referred to as "workers' universities," and many liberal academics would have applauded their existence. In truth, the best of them are far superior in their ability to educate than are many lower-tier public and private diploma mills. They teach competence, and they are cost effective. While the top-tier corporate learning centers are often intended for the top rank personnel of a company, many others (such as those at McDonald's and Motorola) also include a good deal of rank-and-file training.

Corporate universities also differ from academic ones in the age ranges they serve. Many companies are extending their facilities for the care and preschool education of their employees' children. Some are also helping with the care of employees' elderly parents. Recently, 109 companies formed a $25 million partnership aimed at making major improvements in the quality and supply of preschool and elderly care. It operates in forty-four locations from California to Vermont and includes companies like Allstate, AT&T, Exxon, IBM, Kodak, Motorola, and Xerox.

EVEN SMALL COMPANIES DO IT

In the world of business, lifelong learning is something everyone is being urged to do. The kicker is that even mom-and-pop stores do it. For decades no one thought that firms with fewer than one hundred employees and less than $100 million in sales had any education going on, certainly not formal training. That, too, is beginning to change. Smart small companies do train.[5]

A good example of a small company that trains is the Print and Copy Factory in San Francisco. The training has two tracks, one for machine maintenance and repair, the other for selling and general management. The Tattered Cover Book Store in Denver, Colorado, has a formal two-week sales program. The Plumley Companies, automotive suppliers in Tennessee with sales of $80 million, teach rubber technology, statistical process control for quality, and even the Japanese language. Wabash National in Lafayette, Indiana, won an Entrepreneur of the Year award from *Inc.* magazine partly for the attention it pays to training.

Some education-intensive small companies focus on quality and customer service. Cooperative Home Care Associates, a $4 million home-health-care company in the Bronx, New York, the retailer Crate & Barrel, the printer Quad/Graphics, and the service company Lettuce Entertain You Enterprises are all examples. Other learning-oriented small businesses include the Chicago-based Dudek Manufacturing Company, a producer of metal clasps and parts for autos and appliances, which spends 5 percent of payroll on training; and printed circuit board maker Solectron, in Milpitas, California, which won a Baldrige Award for small companies in 1991. It spends on average ninety-five hours per year in learning-intensive exercises.

One thing that often holds small companies back in this area is that they see education and training as an expense taking money away from the bottom line. Don Surber is the president of Accurate Threaded Fasteners, Inc. (ATF), a midwestern supplier of screws and bolts to major corporations in the automotive and telecommunications industries. He has a 7 percent profit margin on $30 million in revenues. ATF employs about two hundred people, mostly immigrants, who speak twelve different languages and have very different skill levels. Each employee goes through an average of seventy-five hours of training in English, math, and reading blueprints in a program that costs the company half a million dollars a year, or 25 percent of ATF profits.

The question for businesses like ATF is whether this cost can be built into the product or priced as a service. Surber believes that in the future, his company is more likely to transform training from an expense to a revenue producer by extending application engineering education to its customers. Such shifts in learning, from cost to revenue producer and from employee to customer, will be major reasons for business's future dominance in education.

Even very small companies will move in this direction. Tabra, Inc., a $3.7 million jewelry maker in Novato, California, teaches English as a second language. Unitech Composite, Inc., which manufactures composite parts for aircraft, partners with Boeing and DuPont to get its training materials. MicroMentor, a $3 million software designer in Cambridge, Massachusetts, sets up learning teams to systematize its on-the-job learning.

Little is heard about small company education efforts because they tend to be informal and are confined to on-the-job training. Sometimes these small businesses ride on the coattails of a large company training program, the way Unitech does. Another method is to meet in informal groups, as MicroMentor does. This means there is no budget line item for training, but if you ask any employee, you'll find training is important and valued. Some small company owners concerned about creating growth environments for key employees typically will permit a day per week or 10 percent of the employees' time for education, reading, or other self-improvement activities. While informal, this often adds up to more than the formal 6.5 percent of revenue spent at Arthur Andersen. The challenge for small companies is to find inexpensive ways to gain the training that is directly useful to the task at hand.

HEAL THYSELF THROUGH LEARNING

Traditional academics who are critics of corporate America are appalled at the notion that business has a responsibility to educate. They question what will happen to all the people who have no job to be trained for or who are laid off. If business can't manage itself better, how is it ever going to manage education?

The most innovative corporate learning sometimes comes, in fact, not from the companies that are healthy, but from those that are recovering. Old dinosaurs fighting extinction may learn quicker and better than competitors blinded by success. There is nothing like facing mortality, even in the corporate form, to focus your attention. General Motors has had an education and training function since 1930. For over fifty years it focused on dealers, never on its own management. It took record losses before the company decided to try new approaches. It instituted programs to orient new hires into the world's largest company and developed leadership programs that all 4,500 top managers had to attend.

More significant—and this is a medicine that other ailing dinosaurs are taking—GM moved learning away from conventional education and training departments. Chevrolet now focuses its instruction on a dozen cross-functional work teams. How to launch the Camaro is taught not in class, but in a team in the field, where headquarters managers are also represented. Oldsmobile is hoping to celebrate its one hundredth birthday in 1997—*if* its cross-functional learning teams of Saturn-Oldsmobile-Chevrolet are successful. Sears Roebuck, another case of past successes turned sour, is following a similar evolution to a new learning path.

Xerox is hardly an ailing dinosaur, but it lost over 50 percent of its market share to Japanese competition. It too had an education facility of which it was proud, but it was stuck in a training department with a mentality like a school. Xerox chairman Paul Allaire rechristened it a "university" in 1992 and expanded its scope to include Xerox's customers. Since Xerox calls itself "the document company," it calls its corporate university "Xerox Document University." While the name sounds flat, it contains a logic that is anything but. Xerox's university has become central to its main business. Currently used by more than twelve thousand employees yearly, it is widely credited with having played a significant role in Xerox's recovery from the devastating competition from Japan.

Xerox PARC (Palo Alto Research Center) is even more keen on inventing new learning approaches. In a widely read article, "Research That Reinvents the Corporation,"[6] PARC's chief scientist, John Seely Brown, demonstrated that corporate research into the education and training of employees had an even greater potential for return on investment than traditional research into new products. People at PARC should know. They invented the mouse and user-friendly interface that Apple, not Xerox, had the smarts to incorporate into the Macintosh. Xerox fumbled the future once not because it couldn't invent a new product, but because it couldn't learn how to commercialize it. PARC is determined not to let that happen again.

PARC's new product is the Live Board, which integrates voice, movies, and drawings onto giant five-by-five-foot screens that can communicate with each other in many locations. Operated by an infrared laser pen that writes in electronic ink, the Live Board can respond to gestures that you make with the laser beam. For a teacher used to a blackboard, or an executive at a flip chart, this is a dream come true. You can circle what you write, move it, reorder your outline, or store it page by page on an infinitely expandable white board. Live Board is part of PARC's attempt to make a knowledge product that itself enhances the learning process.

It was not the training department that created the intelligence for developing or marketing Live Board. Learning and training at PARC occurs in teams that come from across the corporation and beyond. Xerox operates a thirty-year-old strategic alliance with Fuji in Japan. For one of the first times, the corporate parent invited Fuji-Xerox to join the team to develop further and to market Live Board. "You can close the Document University in Virginia," one executive said. "The learning takes place across the company, not on an isolated campus."

IBM is hardly an old dinosaur, either. Overnight it has become a neodinosaur. For decades its employee practices and education were standards by which others judged themselves. IBM's education centers, such as at Thornwood, New York, and La Hulpe, Belgium, were the most technologically advanced and some of the best in business. IBM has spun off its education and training functions in the same spirit that its CEO may split up its business units into several independent entities. The three training and education units IBM spun off are Eduquest, which sells to the K–12 educators; ACIS, which sells to higher education; and Skill Dynamics, which sells management development.

Skill Dynamics operates 48 educational centers and 240 learning centers for self-directed learning. Its sales in 1991 were $400 million internally and $100 million to other companies. The external sales market is growing at 20 percent per year, and its near-term goal is to have more external sales than internal. Skill Dynamics teaches leadership training, conducts classes in "Corporate Workforce Solutions," and offers a master's degree in accounting. It draws faculty members from junior colleges and universities, including Harvard, Stanford, and Wharton. It does all the management training for companies like Montgomery Elevator. It also has a curriculum for quality training, plus training for sales and service people.

But Skill Dynamics has a lot of catching up to do. When companies use education so extensively that it becomes part of their culture, if the company ceases to perform, their education activities will follow suit. Education at IBM, for all its majesty, sometimes seems to be an end in itself and no more dynamic than the parent. Its competitors Electronic Data Systems and Deltec, for example, are 95 percent technology based. In contrast, Skill Dynamics is 80 percent instructor led. It's odd that a company spun off from the world's fallen technology leader never learned how to use its *own* technology to lead in business.

INVESTING IN OUR FUTURE

The corporate average spent on employee education is about 1.5 percent of payroll, a little over 1 percent of gross revenues, and .75 percent of the GNP.[7] Estimates of total annual spending range from $30 billion to $70 billion. No one knows for sure, but most agree that the total is probably a lot higher than is currently estimated.

Large companies with over five thousand employees are the most visible and spend around 2 percent of payroll. Some small companies with one hundred employees or fewer also engage in education and training, but most of it is informal and on the job, seldom counted in the overall figures on employee education.

Furthermore, the estimates typically do not include indirect costs, such as the cost of employees' wages and benefits while they are studying, or fixed costs such as building construction or classroom depreciation. They also exclude the costs of that ever-illusive informal on-the-job training (OJT), without which employees would fall behind in their knowledge or, in the case of formal training sessions, be away from their jobs too long. On-the-job training is seldom accounted for financially. There are few measurements for estimating the costs of informal learning by experience, by osmosis, and just by being in the workplace. If all of these additional items were factored in, estimates of the amount spent annually on employee education could range as high as $200 billion.[8]

President Clinton wanted all but the smallest companies to invest 1.5 percent of their payroll in educating their workforce or to pay an equivalent amount as a training tax. Along with many other parts of his economic plan, that goal fell in the first few months of his administration. If it did take place, opponents said, it would put a number of companies out of business and cost $30 billion from our $2 trillion–plus private sector payroll. This is equivalent only to about 7 percent of what we currently spend on all K–college education and is perplexing because business already spends that much, or more, of the target figure. The anomaly is due to the difference between interpreting 1.5 percent as the average or as the minimum required. Either that or no one has the numbers right.

Management guru Tom Peters would up the ante even farther. He urges all companies to recognize training as a research and development expenditure, fund it as a percent of gross revenues (not just of payroll), and double the number to 3 percent.[9] Since gross revenues are about double payroll, or $4 trillion, jumping to 3 percent would yield four times the earlier figure and would create an employee education market of about $120 billion, or almost 30 percent of today's K–college market. Although such an expenditure is even less likely to occur, as advocacy, many think it is not going overboard.

One problem with such programs is how to create the incentives that would make carrying them out worthwhile. Passing federal legislation that allows corporations a deductible expense for the depreciation of human capital would help considerably. It would offer companies an incentive to invest in maintaining and developing their human assets through continuing education. It would also enhance our international competitiveness.

Employers resist training programs because they don't want to invest in resources that might walk out the door immediately after a large dollop of training, before the benefits of the investment can be realized. Manufacturers in the United States have a 40 percent turnover rate, for example, compared with 25 percent in Germany and 18 percent in Japan. An accelerated depreciation schedule would reduce this risk. An even greater depreciation credit to compensate companies for those who do leave this way would reduce the risk even more.

If anything, most people in the private sector believe that the pace of change in their business will increase, indicating a greater need for employee and customer learning in order to keep up. A doubling every decade, on average, is a reasonable prediction. People getting trained one week per year (forty hours) now, at the beginning of their forty-year careers, might find this increasing through the decades to a day per month, a month per year, and perhaps even a day per week by the time they retire in the 2030s. At that rate we will indeed be learning a living.

Lifelong learning is creating new market segments, expanding the realm of who gets educated and by whom. Employee education is a growing area, and one that is currently better served by business than by business schools. Business schools, like the education system in general, are locked in the old paradigm. When customer education, the next great learning segment, is added, we have to realize that business is already a very significant educator and is on its way to becoming *the* major force in education.

CHAPTER 5

THE *LAST* THING YOU WANT IS A LEARNING ORGANIZATION

When the rate of change outside
exceeds the rate of change inside,
the end is in sight.

—JACK WELCH, chairman and CEO,
General Electric

ORGANIZATIONITIS

Learning organizations are very much in vogue. Many senior executives, consultants, and human resources departments are striving to make their companies learning organizations. It sounds right, but it isn't. The *last* thing you want to grow is a learning organization. First you need to grow a learning business. You do not want to grow an organization for a business that does not yet exist. Until you truly have a learning business and know what this means in intimate detail, you cannot possibly know what kind of an organization you will need to run and support it. If you really want your company to have a learning organization,[1] make certain that it is already becoming a learning business.

A learning business today is not one that is learning how to use data or information. Those were learning businesses generations ago, in the 1960s and 1980s, respectively. *A learning business today is one that leverages the economic value of knowledge.* It is always figuring out how to define, acquire, develop, apply, measure, grow, use, multiply, protect, transfer, sell, profit by, and celebrate the company's know-how. And it may be know-how about developing new products, about serving customers, about any number of things.

True learning organizations cannot exist until we have the growth of learning businesses—that is, companies that base their market value and price their offerings in terms of the value their knowledge brings. Knowledge technology is becoming central to all businesses. It has been decades in the making and still has another decade or more to go before it matures. In the process, the defining characteristics of the organization of these businesses will emerge. The true learning organization is always consequence, never cause; you will always find its contours in the landscape of the business. You have to learn how to see them.

To draw well, artists have to learn how to see. Or, to draw well, you have to learn to see like an artist. When artists draw faces they don't see noses, ears, and mouths. They see lines, angles, and shadows. When they draw a chair, they draw not the legs, but the spaces around and between the legs. Artists call this the *negative space*. To create a learning organization, you have to see the negative spaces in which it resides, and then the contours of the organization will emerge. To build a true learning organization, let it emerge in response to the contours of the knowledge business you are building.

If you do this, you might find that you want a teaching organization at least as much as a learning organization. Why, then, do most businesses focus on learning organizations and learning curves and not on teaching organizations and teaching curves? The CEOs who say "I want to make my company into a learning organization!" are treated as enlightened executives. But if they were to proclaim "I want to make my company into a teaching organization!" people would think they were crazy. Why is one highly prized in business and not the other?

Teaching is a producer good, while learning is initially a consumer activity. The former is given, the latter received. Teaching takes what you've learned and systematically imparts it to others. It spreads and multiplies something that is deemed worth sharing. Learning, by contrast, is acquisitive, either through instruction, study, or experience. Individuals consume learning, but there is no guarantee that they will give back more than they take in.

Producing more than we consume, whether as individuals or as corporations, is the hallmark of productivity. True learning businesses, therefore, must also be teaching businesses, imparting to their customers the additional value of learning together with the product or service offered. Similarly, true learning organizations must also be teaching organizations, imparting to their employees some quotient of growth beyond their current capacities.

As business migrates toward the economic value of knowledge, as both provider and consumer, its organizations will move in the same direction. The characteristics of these organizations, therefore, seem certain: a focus on service and productivity—increasingly fast, flexible, customized, networked, and global.

EVERY BUSINESS WILL ORGANIZE AROUND SERVICES

Three-quarters of the value added in today's economy comes from services. Service businesses represent three-quarters of the private sector's roughly ninety million jobs in the economy, and many of the remainder are actually service jobs disguised within nonservice companies. In the years ahead, the ways service businesses organize will dominate all economic activity, not only the service businesses themselves. Just as the organization of service businesses in the industrial economy reflected manufacturing-based models of organization, the reverse will now be true. Even the organization of manufacturing businesses will look increasingly like service-based organizations. Education and learning are services and will be organized as such, whether provided internally to employees or externally to customers.

Product businesses, as they too add value based on knowledge, will imitate organizing principles from service businesses. More important, they will come to think of themselves as service businesses, and this shift will be the greater reason for them to organize differently. Companies won't reorganize themselves because they say "How can we organize like a service business?" Grafting service organizations onto companies that are not yet service businesses won't work. The companies that try it will find themselves engaging in expensive, time-consuming, and frustrating exercises in failed attempts at organizational change.

What will happen is that as their business looks more and more like a service business, the characteristics of the organization will shift imperceptibly to reflect this, and a service organization will be the outcome. Chevrolet, in the context of its Total Customer Enthusiasm initiative, can learn more from service organizations like Federal Express or Disney than from organizations in the same industrial business, like Ford. Having the organization reflect the actual business more accurately will help companies move in the direction of the value of knowledge and organizing around it.

Recently one of us was leading a group of thirty Western businesspeople through Japan to learn about Japanese management techniques. We took the bullet train from Hiroshima to Osaka, and since the train stopped for only twenty seconds in Hiroshima, it would have been impossible to get all the executives and their luggage on the train at the same time. So we hired a trucking company and crew to transfer the luggage separately. The crew carefully removed all luggage from each individual's room in Hiroshima and placed it in his pre-checked-in room in another chain's hotel in Osaka. Can you imagine doing that in the United States and ever seeing your luggage again?

One of the executives, thinking his shoes were too worn, had discarded them in the wastepaper basket in his Hiroshima hotel room. Imagine his shock when he entered his room in Osaka and saw his old shoes carefully laid in the wastepaper basket there. Was the Japanese trucking company politely saying that these shoes still had life and should not yet be thrown away, or was the company accommodating a crazy foreigner who liked to keep his shoes in the wastepaper basket? Either way, the company was organized for highly intelligent service at every level.

The ascendancy of services in our economy was not recognized until the 1970s, although manufacturing had reached its high-water mark in the 1950s and was on the decline. For twenty years skeptics thought services added less value to the economy than did manufacturing, were the least capital-intensive sector, and were the domain of small shops and low-wage jobs. In fact, the service sector was following the same progression and evolution as the agrarian and manufacturing sectors.

As the agricultural sector aged, it shrank as a proportion of the total economy. It also became the most capital intensive. Manufacturing is headed in the same direction, shrinking in size and right behind agriculture in its aggressive use of capital. The service sector is still at an early stage of growth, but as it matures it, too, will evolve along the same path and become much more capital intensive.

With maturity has come increased scale. *Fortune*'s Service 500 list, for example, contributed 1.2 million new jobs, or 17 percent of total job growth, between 1986 and 1991. Capital investment per "information worker" has also increased and, according to Stephen Roach, chief economist of Morgan Stanley, now surpasses that for workers in basic industry.[2]

PRODUCTIVITY-BASED ORGANIZATIONS

Businesses have been working smarter, achieving greater productivity with fewer employees. Economists speak of the sputtering recovery from the most recent recession as "productivity led," meaning that the significant gains in output occurred without hiring many new workers. In 1992, for example, productivity was up 2.8 percent, the highest in twenty years, but the number of jobs kept shrinking.

Since organization follows business, it also follows that businesses with smart products and services will require smart workers and organizational forms to accommodate them. It took the first quarter of this economy just to recognize the importance of services, then the second quarter for the vast majority of jobs to be redefined as service work. In this mature, third part of the cycle, the current emphasis is on improving the quality and value of the dominant service sector and on making organizations productive. This is where the emergence of knowledge-based businesses will play a major role, setting the stage, finally, for smart workers and for knowledge-based organizations to reflect and run them. Corporate labs like Xerox PARC and AT&T Bell Labs, and government labs like Los Alamos National Laboratory, are run as knowledge-based organizations. When knowledge spreads out of the labs, it may well carry with it their methods of organization.

Because service work has been labor intensive and labor is treated as a variable cost in the capitalist system, it has historically been first to experience cuts when the pinch comes. Downsizing and the euphemistic "rightsizing" were the first steps taken to improve performance. This was followed quickly by the notion that simply reducing bloat was not enough, that the very organization of work itself had to be rethought. The halting recovery from the last recession differed from previous comebacks in that not all laid-off workers were put back to work.

This led to the next development, business process reengineering, spearheaded by Michael Hammer and James Champy.[3] The word is a misnomer. The prefix "re-" means backward, to do something over again or to restore it to an original or former state, and anything but this is happening. Also, engineering is generally associated with technology and the R&D and manufacturing functions. Yet business process reengineering is about organization; despite the fact that it is a backward-looking term for a forward-looking notion, it provides another indication of what smart, learning, and knowledgeable organizations will look like.

Presently only about 15 percent of manufacturing companies and less than 5 percent of service companies have been through a reengineering process. Services have been slower to adapt because engineer types and service types don't couple naturally. More important, output and quality are difficult to measure, although such measurement is a prerequisite for sustainable change. Despite the relatively small numbers, however, leading companies such as BancOne, Ford, Motorola, and Xerox have demonstrated major productivity gains with these techniques, and now the approach has snowballed.

Business process reengineering uses engineering concepts to redefine the flow of work and results in modifying or abandoning practices that were at the heart of organization in an industrial framework. The division of labor, specialization, and hierarchy are downplayed in favor of such techniques as working in teams, training people in multiple tasks and skills, flattening the hierarchy, and pushing decision making as far down as possible. Emphasis is on speeding up and simplifying the work flow and on eliminating jobs that do not add measurable value. In industrial age lingo, there is no more staff, because after the cuts everyone produces direct, measurable, and marketable value. The Los Alamos Lab, for example, combined four management levels into one, and twenty-seven division leaders all equal in rank now report to the director.

An excellent way to achieve this is to require all support staff to sell some of their services in the marketplace, outside the company. Between 20 and 40 percent would be a good number. If that is not possible, then the service staff is probably not up to the job, and the service should be contracted for from outside. This is part of the logic that led IBM to spin off those thousands of full-time educators and support staff, who now must survive from a mix of clients both inside and outside the company.

Even if part of an organization does produce value, does it produce better value than any similar part in other organizations?

In other words, is it "best in the world" at what it does? Because of the complexity and interrelatedness of business today, no one can excel at everything. There is a school of thought, often identified with such phrases as "back to basics," "stick to the knitting," and "core competencies," advocating that companies should pick the few things they do better than anyone else, concentrate their energies there, and outsource everything else to companies that are best in the world in doing each of those things.[4]

This leaves a lean and leveraged organization, involved in an enormous number of alliances, partnerships, and consortia to supply the variety of functions and activities it has gotten rid of but nevertheless still needs. The European companies ABB and IKEA are striking examples of this trend. Businesses built around core competencies lead to core organizations. Everything else goes outside. It stays attached, of course, but from outside. Central to the idea is that only organizations pared to their essential core will remain nimble enough to keep pace with the speed of new technologies and, simultaneously, broad enough to respond to variety and complexity.

NETWORKED ORGANIZATIONS

These are networked businesses, and they need networked organizations to run them. The ability to work with a multitude of linkages, connections, partnerships, and alliances will be an important part of an organization's job and value. We are in the era of *inter-*: interactive, intermedia, international, and interorganization. Over the next two decades, commentaries and concerns about *inter*organization matters will come to get as much attention as internal (*intra-*) ones. Saturn calls the ultimate car buyer a "customer," and everyone else, from supplier to dealer to assembly line worker, is an intraorganizational "partner."

If the rate of organization change has to keep up with the rate of business change, and this, in turn, with the rate of technological change, then the organization is going to be in such constant turmoil that the old models will not work. We cannot simply adjust the current way we organize and exhort those inside to accommodate themselves. The required pace is just too great. No sooner will people have adjusted to a new way of doing things than those things will be changed on them again. Most likely they will not even have adjusted before another change comes through.

A friend at a large telecommunications company was the victim of the fourth reorganization in two years. She moved with her department from New Jersey to Colorado, only to find that her new department had been eliminated. Now she owns houses in both states and faces involuntary early retirement. Her case is not unique.

The result of such constant modification is not exhilaration. It is more like chaos and confusion, with very high stress, low morale, and a sense of "Why bother, it's going to change yet again anyway." Reorganization becomes the steady state. *Plus ça change . . .* The corollary is that the organization, in fact, does not change sufficiently and so falls behind. Neither adjustment is acceptable, and fundamentally new methods will evolve.

The larger the organization, the less willing and/or able it will be to abandon what it is currently doing and actually transform itself into something that it is not. Because smaller organizations generally are more flexible and quicker to react than large ones, rapid technological change favors designs that keep organizations small enough to be quick yet large enough to have leverage.

This is compatible with keeping head count down and is an even more important reason for downsizing and outsourcing than is cost savings or strategic focus. It is also compatible with the elimination of middle layers that are replaced by information flows. Data flows only automated the old way of doing things, adding duplication more often than productivity. Information flows redesigned rather than duplicated, and we now see productivity increases beginning to show. As we put the information flows in our organizations to productive use, knowledge flows will accelerate and we can expect another round of restyling in search of the knowledge organization.

THE QUEST FOR FAST ORGANIZATIONS

On a recent business trip to Hong Kong, a globe-trotting friend of ours stopped first in Los Angeles for a night's sleep. When she entered the lobby at the well-known American chain hotel, no one was at the front desk. She waited several minutes before someone came, all smiles, to check her in. Unfortunately he assigned her a room that was occupied, so she returned to the lobby to get another room. This time she got a key that didn't work and had to go back down again. Finally she got settled in her room, but the luggage failed to show up because the bellhop was still trying to deliver it to the person in the first room. Now two guests were angry. The next morning she wrote a note to the manager. *Three months later* she got a reply: "We're so sorry. I hope this incident doesn't deter you from staying at our hotel in the future." The manager is hoping in vain.

In Hong Kong our friend went to a hotel run by a well-known Asian chain. She checked in, got her room, hung out the "Do Not Disturb" sign, and promptly hit the sack to overcome jet lag. She had an early morning meeting and left her room after a few hours' sleep but forgot to remove the sign. It stayed there all day long, and the maid was perplexed: how was she to make up the room? Between the business meetings and dinner, it was after 11:00 P.M. when our friend returned to the hotel. A young woman intercepted her as she stepped from the elevator. "I'm so sorry your room is not made up," she said. "We saw the sign and had to respect your wishes. Would you like your room made up now?"

"Please do," said our friend, trying to figure out how she had been recognized. The hallway cleaning team had her room ready in under four minutes, complete with turned-down bed and a fresh orchid and chocolate on the pillow.

Which hotel would you stay in again? The one organized for smart and fast service or the one run with dumb and slow service?

Fast is about time. At the turn of the century, Einstein made us aware of time as an intrinsic dimension of the universe. Time has recently become intrinsic to business as well and over the years has been transformed from a fixed restraint to managed resource. Frederick Taylor's time-and-motion studies of almost a century ago were an early example of this transformation. Today business has wholeheartedly embraced the concept that time is money. Time-based competition is now a pillar of business strategy. In a survey of its top executives, DuPont put creativity and time-based competition as its top priorities.

In all, it took almost a century before business truly came to the realization that time is a leverageable resource. This was made possible by computer technology: business machines became so fast that the response to input became faster as well; this necessitated immediate updates, which in turn affected subsequent inputs, thereby guiding the process. This development came to be known as real-time processing, a great advance during the data phase of this information era. In simpler terms, real-time processing is our ability to affect things while they're happening rather than after the fact. It makes you wonder what kind of time business operated in before it grasped the power of operating in real time. When you operate in real time you can affect outcomes. If you're quick enough, you can guide your destiny.

In business, fast is about how little time you take to accomplish something, establishing a norm or standard and then exceeding it. It's about a decade of growth, annual returns, quarterly profits, monthly sales figures, weekly reports, daily schedules, miles per hour, products per minute, and millions of instructions per second. In business, speed equals wealth. Your ability to move *from concept to customer* faster than your competition has become a major advantage.

A fast business starts with a vision or concept and moves it through the value chain to a customer quicker and better than anyone else. It determines where in the chain the value added is the greatest, and that is where they wring time out. The benchmark for a fast business is a relevant comparison with the competition. Xerox, for example, requires all employees, from production worker and secretary to top executive, to measure their performance against peers in at least two other competing companies.

Fast businesses require fast organizations to run them. But fast organizations are almost oxymorons. Where they do exist, they change as rapidly as their businesses. The real difficulty is not in defining a fast organization, it is in making it happen. People who try to build learning organizations invariably spend too much time building an organization and too little time building the business. The focus is wrong. You should never expend less than two-thirds of your energies on your business and never more than one-third of your energies on your organization. Otherwise you have a business that exists to carry out an organization. This is bureaucracy.

Typical actions in the organization of a learning business often include changing the dress code, eliminating named parking spots, and closing the executive dining room. The idea is to reduce hierarchy and encourage the free exchange of knowledge. These are laudable goals and reasonable steps, but by themselves they are unlikely to change more deeply rooted patterns of thought and behavior. Reducing the number of reporting levels and creating cross-functional teams are other organization actions. They are not wrong, in and of themselves. They make sense. But they fail when they are the dominant focus and the desired result. Fewer reporting levels will not produce a knowledge-based business, but a functioning knowledge-based business will have little hierarchy.

The next time you are in a meeting in your company, time how long the group can talk without discussing something about the organization. We've been in many meetings where this can be measured in seconds, let alone minutes. Establish a time limit, and if the talk returns prematurely to organization, literally blow the whistle by sounding a buzzer or a beeper. People who say "uhm," "like," or "you know" in every sentence don't stop until they become aware of just how often they do it. The same is true for those suffering from organizationitis. The first couple of beeps may be awkward and slow up discussion, but people catch on fast.

Building a fast organization involves identifying the key work flow that directly adds customer value and then performing it better than anyone else. Paradoxically, these tasks often take no more than 5 or 6 percent of the total time spent. Nevertheless, the organization must be structured around a continuous flow between these key links, and everything else should be done off-line or outsourced. Fast organizations will be as large as necessary and as small as possible. Like computer chips, they will shrink in size while they grow in value. The recipe for action is simple: *Change your organization as fast as your business changes—and no slower.*

FLEXIBILITY IN PEOPLE AND IN ORGANIZATIONS

An industrial age machine that stamps out thousands of identical widgets every minute is fast but not flexible. If these machines were reset to alter each widget ever so slightly, they would be flexible, but costly and not fast. Today's computer technology, however, can reset specifications instantaneously, allowing the machine to be both fast and flexible and for virtually the same cost as with straight runs. Business has learned to be both fast and flexible. Organizations have to follow suit.

As the business pace accelerates and companies come out of the last recession, rather than rehiring to replenish their ranks, many are turning to contract labor. This is done specifically for cost containment, to avoid the additional one-quarter to one-third of payroll expenses and even more expensive benefits. Health benefits alone are 14 percent of payroll expenses. Just as there is no question that this causes burdens to nonemployees on contract, there is also no doubt that it makes the organization more flexible. Moreover, independent contractors are not generally viewed or treated like full-time company employees, so management is less likely to be patient with those who are not flexible.

At first blush this sounds like a throwback to preunion days. But there is one great difference. The people laid off in previous recessions tended to be at the bottom of the organization, whereas middle-management ranks and professionals were depleted in this one. When workers were laid off in the industrial era, they no longer had the means or the resources to stay productive. In this era, however, with knowledge as the key resource of the economy, white-collar workers are finding that they take this most valuable resource with them when they are laid off. Knowledge resides more in the person than in the organization. This gives people far more flexibility than they ever had in the past. Part of that flexibility is what they bring to creating new enterprise.

When two senior project managers were laid off from Conoco in a downsizing, they used their severance pay as seed money and negotiated a license to lease the results of their project back to Conoco and to sell it to noncompeting outside companies. Corning Glass enables former employees to become independent entrepreneurs by letting them market to outside buyers "shelf technology" it no longer uses.

Organizations, like businesses and other living things, have life cycles. Flexibility is characteristic of the first quarter of an organization's life cycle, and the rest is a tale of increasing rigidity. Organizations are flexible in the beginning because they don't have a choice. New businesses are learning as they go, and the people don't have much time, the need, or resources for organizing. Only when they hit the second quarter, and the business is growing like mad, do they begin to say, "We need more people, we need planning and controls, we need systems and structure. We've got to get some organization here." The organization runs to catch up with the growing business.

In retrospect, these are the halcyon days. At the far end of the cycle, once the business has slowed down, the organization has taken on a life of its own and is still growing. Not only has it caught up, but it has overtaken the business. Companies in the last quarter of their life cycle seem to have businesses that exist to run their organizations, which is an inversion of the true purpose of any institution, whether economic or educational. The organization tail wagging the business dog is a problem that has afflicted all the once great corporations and educational institutions now in crisis.

If organization lags behind business at the beginning of its life cycle and the reverse is true at the end, then somewhere along the way the two must be in balance with one another. That is probably true for a very brief moment, and it marks the shift from growth to maturity. In maturity, like people who accumulate possessions, businesses accumulate organizations.

Short life cycles are a blessing in disguise for mature companies. They force management to change. The longer the business life cycle, the less flexible its organization is going to be. The culture becomes set in its ways. People who have spent their entire career doing things one way are rarely able to make the changes needed and build a new culture. Aging organizations are the least likely to bring on a generation of new businesses. Oil companies like Shell, Chevron, and Arco may not see it that way, but reorganization will be necessary if they hope to prosper in the new knowledge-based economy.

Four decades ago, at the beginning of this current economy, we were entrenched in the period of the "organization man," and self-employment was not a popular route to success. Entrepreneurs were more prominent in an earlier era, when few organizations employed thousands of people. Today both characteristics are present simultaneously: self-employment is highly esteemed once again, and many organizations still have thousands of employees, even after massive downsizing.

Individuals are far more flexible than organizations. While organizations are certainly not static, the rate at which truly new approaches develop seems only to crawl along. The organization man of the 1950s sacrificed flexibility for security. The individual entrepreneur of the 1980s was flexible, but often far from secure. In the 1990s flexibility resides in both the individual and the organization. Organizations will stay flexible by finding ways to measure the productivity and value added by every unit, and they will strive to increase those measures with ever fewer people. Individuals will stay flexible by grasping that today's most sought after resource, knowledge, lies within their own persons, not the organization. And they will find ways to leverage the freedom, power, and wealth that creates.

These attributes will establish themselves first in business, and then, as business moves more and more into learning and education, they will gradually be adopted in schools as well. Some schools will learn to be service oriented, productive, fast, and flexible.

ORGANIZING SMART SCHOOLS FOR LEARNING STUDENTS

Whatever institution runs education organizes it its own way. When church education was the dominant form, schools reflected church approaches to organization. Clergy were teachers, pupils were arranged in neat rows like church pews. Discipline and obedience were primary values. Teachers are in the hire of the institution that runs the schools and, as such, reflect its values. In today's government-run public schools, teachers are civil servants and schools look and are run like government bureaucracies.

If education is redefined and the private sector is responsible for bigger segments, it is naturally going to staff those segments, not with clergy or civil servants, but with people who reflect the values, practices, and organization of enterprise. More education will take place outside formal classrooms, mediated more by technology than by instructors. Much of it will be embedded in products or wrapped around offerings as servicers. It will be available on an as-needed basis, in real time, and tailored to the learners' particular requirements. Just-in-time learning will become as popular as just-in-time manufacturing. Business will organize education and learning according to its own ways.

The pillars of any business are its products and markets. Companies are often distinguished by whether they are product centered or customer driven—that is, whose perspective is considered first and foremost. In the industrial economy the focus was on the products and the grounding was from the provider's point of view. In this economy the focus is on the market and the grounding is the customer's or user's perspective. This shift from product to market focus is also characteristic of the shift that is starting to take place in how education is organized.

Education is a product-focused activity, whereas learning takes the customer's perspective. We speak of educat-*ors,* those who provide the offering, but never of educat-*ees,* those who receive it. According to the dictionary, -*ors* are "noun suffixes denoting do-ers," while -*ees* are "passive" suffixes indicating the object of an action. The -*ors* are the active ones, the focus of attention, doing what needs to be done. The -*ees* are passive recipients, objects, not subjects.

The industrial approach to education embraced this model, making teachers the actors and students the passive recipients. In contrast, the emerging new model takes the market perspective by making students the active players. The active focus will shift from the provider to the user, from educat-*ors* (teachers) to learn-*ors* (students), and *the educating act will reside increasingly in the active learner, rather than in the teacher-manager.* In the new learning marketplace, customers, employees, and students are all active learners or, even more accurately, interactive learners. This is revolutionary—comparable to the unionization of workers in the industrial era to take power from the bosses.

Whoever has the information or knowledge is the educator. It may be the learners themselves, employees or students, engaging directly with their subject, unmediated by bosses and teachers. Or it may be line personnel delivering instruction on the job, supported and coordinated by a full-time certified staff that designs, develops, and evaluates the program. In business-led education, full-time instructors may be less valuable than many part-time instructors with real-time experience. As such, education will have more in common with church-led models than with government-run schools, where part-timers are used because of budget constraints and unfortunately are (usually) of questionable quality and less effective. Either way, the organization of learning in business-led education is tied to specific tasks, emphasizes practicality and measurable results, minimizes intermediaries between the learners and the information, and maximizes the productive use of the resulting knowledge.

In classrooms, the teacher-boss at the front of the room with orderly rows of student-workers learning rote lessons is a thing of the past. Information age classrooms increasingly follow a network model, with small clustered groups linked together fluidly around changing tasks. As learners turn to technology for expertise about content, teachers will focus their expertise more around process and relationships. Again, more responsibility for learning shifts to the learners, who advance as they learn the material rather than by the arbitrary logic of forty-minute periods and twelve-week semesters.

Most of these shifts have already occurred in corporate classrooms filled with employees and customers. Ultimately these practices will find their way into student classrooms as well. The information age power of education is the power over knowledge more than over people. Curiously, the dictionary's first definition of power is the "ability, whether physical, mental, or moral, to act," while "control over others" is second. These two definitions capture very well the power shift between industrial age and information age classrooms.[5] The shift is occurring in the private sector faster than in the public sector. Business organizations adapt to changes more quickly than educational organizations.

When educators use technology merely to do their same old job better, they fail. The private sector initially made this same mistake, but now business is using technology to learn and to educate differently. The private sector is finally focusing on the productive use of information and assessing how knowledge intensive their businesses and organizations are. If one company needs half as many employees as another company to produce a given amount of profits, the first is twice as knowledge intensive as the second. Business will drive education in this same direction, using technology, for example, to increase self-instruction in employee training.

GLOBAL REACH

Education is one of the last institutions to acquire an international or global reach, because historically its focus has been local, state, and national. In country after country, education follows political lines, more than religious, cultural, or economic ones. Government has been far more successful within the geographic limits of the nation-state than it has been with transnational or global arrangements.

In America, with its local traditions, government-led education systems reflect this same outer limit. Even the federal government is routinely ignored by educators, and schools remain one of the last provincial institutions. It is not surprising, therefore, that 60 percent of American high school graduates today cannot find Japan on a globe, and 80 percent cannot distinguish between Stalin and Anwar Sadat. One-quarter of Dallas high schoolers cannot name the country that forms their southern border, and 39 percent in Boston couldn't name the six New England states.[6]

In contrast, business has a global reach. So the more it becomes involved in education, the more we can expect education to act and to organize globally. Globalizing our educational institutions does not simply mean introducing more geography courses into K–8 (although this, too, is needed). First, it will mean changing the infrastructure of our strongest offerings, the higher levels of education, from domestic to global undertakings. Changing attitudes and practices about the import and export of education is a good example of how this can occur.

Students from abroad are flooding into American graduate schools. Over 36,500 Japanese students are enrolled in American colleges and universities. In contrast, under 1,500 American students are studying in Japan. If the financial trade figures were this unbalanced, our deficit with Japan would be twenty-five times greater than it is. We label this trend as another example of our trade imbalance, seeing problems instead of opportunities. Instead we should interpret the increased numbers of international students as an opportunity to globalize what is best about our educational system. We should export our higher education and re-create its successful model abroad.

Of the total number of doctoral degrees earned in America in 1972, 15 percent were awarded to noncitizens; in 1989 the proportion increased to 26 percent and will likely continue on that same trajectory. In science and technology courses, non-U.S. citizens now earn over half of the advanced degrees awarded annually. According to the American Mathematical Society, 57 percent of the 933 mathematics doctorates awarded in 1989 went to non-Americans. At some schools the numbers are even more lopsided. At the New Jersey Institute of Technology, for example, 83 percent of the full-time students and 73 percent of the graduate students are from Asia.

The greater concern to Americans, however, is not that there are so many foreigners, but that so few American students are applying and enrolling for advanced degrees. The youth of America, the experts argue, have not received adequate training or motivation throughout their lives, from kindergarten through college, particularly in technology and science. While there is merit to this point of view, it does not lead to a resolution of the problem as it is being defined. Perhaps a more constructive approach is to see this trend as part of a well-documented evolution in the maturation of an industry—in this case, education. In enterprise, markets evolve from local to national, then to global competition. When the rate of growth in a domestic market shrinks, companies look abroad for new growth. Universities are doing the same thing in many ways. Schools are finding graduate student customers from abroad for their offerings.

The first phase of international growth is usually by export. This is happening in education: most students from abroad return home. The next phase is foreign direct manufacture, and we should expect a similar development in the internationalization of education. As students from developing countries return home from training in developed ones, their countries will begin local production of the goods (that is, of the knowledge workers) they had previously imported. If a business lets this happen, it loses its foreign market to local producers of equal caliber. To prevent this, manufacturers stop exporting and shift instead to direct competition. They set up their factories and offices in those economies.

Education will and should follow a similar path, setting up schools of higher learning abroad. One way for a country to sustain its competitive advantage is by moving directly into the global arena the very part of the educational sector in which it has the greatest global competence. Dartmouth already has a campus in Japan, Tufts a school in Italy, and 1,200 American colleges and universities have institutionally sponsored study-abroad programs. The same is true for Japan, which has schools in Australia, Canada, and the United States. Britain and France have long had universities in Africa and Asia.

Nevertheless, these efforts pale in comparison with corporations. KPMG Peat Marwick has teaching facilities in sixty countries. AT&T has programs for employees and customers from over fifty countries. McDonald's Hamburger University trains employees in sixty-five countries and has hardwired simultaneous translation facilities for eighteen languages into its main American campus. Its training program for Russians and for Americans in Russia is tops. Harvard Business School, which did not have a single foreign-language newspaper on its library's periodical table until 1992, could learn a thing or two from Hamburger University.

During the next decades we should see many more strategic alliances between American universities and their counterparts abroad, where the American partners contract to build and run academic enterprises in the areas of their most distinctive competence. In the same way that the private sector has come to replace American managers abroad with equally well trained local managers, universities can staff these global branches with the very foreign graduates they have previously trained.

Following the logic of evolution from local to national to global activity leads to a far more heretical possibility: strategic alliances with K–12 educational systems from abroad to teach science and technology courses here. In the same way that we know how to produce the world's best centers of higher education, and ought to export and then foreign direct manufacture this skill, other countries know how to do things better than we do at earlier levels of education.

Perhaps there is an American school system here that is global enough in its thinking to forge an alliance with a Korean school system to teach our youngsters math, or a Japanese school system to teach technology, or a British or German school system to teach science. There are always cultural explanations about why some practices work in one national venue and not another. Nonetheless, when the sovereignty and isolation of industrial order nation-states yield to a more interlinked global order of world trading regions, we should start thinking along the same lines for our educational institutions.

Our society operates in an ever more interconnected world, and general education at the earliest levels should reflect this. Russian math textbooks for grades one through three and Japanese math textbooks for grades seven through nine have been published in English. Americans, whether in high school, college, or adult education, would have difficulty meeting the high standards of these books. The point is *not* that these standards were produced by governments and therefore American versions should be, too. Business more than government, however, uses real world-class standards to survive. Whether the public or private route is taken, the point is that achieving world-class standards means globalizing the organization of education at all levels. Local communities that are considering privatization of parts of their general education system should consider partnerships with sometimes superior educational systems of sister cities abroad.

In the European Community, supranational education policies are being established that allow study from a French university to be credited in a German one. A teacher hired to teach science in an English secondary school has the right to be considered for a job at a French lycée (high school). Translate this into an American context. The United States has entered into the North American Free Trade Agreement with Mexico and Canada. Pressures similar to those experienced by the EC are bound to arise to create an educational policy to cover interrelationships among Mexican, American, and Canadian schools. Should doctors trained to teach in Guadalajara be routinely considered for positions at McGill Medical School in Toronto? Should language work in Monterey,

California, be credited at the University of Monterrey, Mexico?

Questions like these are difficult to answer. The point is not whether we react positively or negatively to any specific one of them. Rather, the point is that our government-run education system does not and will not have a global reach, whereas business must have one and will therefore pass it on to education. So it, too, will become networked, fast, flexible, and customized and will focus on service and productivity.

CHAPTER 6

THE SIX R's

Don't let your schooling interfere with your education.

—MARK TWAIN

THE IMPACT OF BUSINESS ON SCHOOLS

Reading, 'riting, and religion were the original three R's. Religion was lopped off when church was separated from state, and 'rithmetic was added when public schooling was established.

Reform is another R word. Radical reform is definitely needed in our schools, but the old education system cannot fulfill our future learning needs. It is like trying to make a hundred-year-old schoolhouse energy efficient. You can rehab, reinsulate, recaulk, and reshutter it, but the final result will still be quite different from a school designed and built from the outset to maximize energy efficiency. For all the energy and money that will be spent on improving our ailing K–12 public schools, no complete cure will be found. Some progress will be made improving the old system, but like the building itself, these rehabs will not be as effective as creating new ways of educating.

Since the current system cannot be torn down, however, it does have to be fixed. Revitalizing our public school system is absolutely essential. But it is an essential short-term effort, not a long-term solution. While enormous sums of talent and money will yield a few notable successes, the system itself will remain pretty much the same and, therefore, never quite adequate to current needs.

A few vehement critics say our school system is dead and should be cast away to make room for the new approaches, but they are romantics more than revolutionaries. While generally accurate in their criticism of what's wrong, they tend to be hopelessly naive in an intemperate haste to tear down the old before the new is ready. What are students to do during the period between the failed school system of a past age and the kind of learning that will prevail in the future? There are still jobs to train for, families to feed. Until new ways of learning mature inside adult markets, it is foolish to suggest that business play the dominant role in transforming K–12 public schools. Schools probably will be revived in the same manner as other institutions and industries in the final years of their life cycle.

Here's what's likely to happen. The old schools will keep chugging along, losing adherents and popularity, as people turn increasingly to alternative sources of education. New entrants into the education marketplace, such as Chris Whittle's stillborn Edison Project, will make inroads only in selective niches. The weakest dinosaurs will collapse. The survivors will scale way back. Public schools will stop trying to be all things educational to all citizens. Like steel and other basic industries, those who succeed in transforming themselves do so only by becoming smaller, more focused, and very agile in the limited markets they choose to serve.

After another decade or two, this is the path that public education will ultimately take. It won't happen sooner, because the new alternatives for other segments of the education market already have to be in place. Business will focus first on nonschool segments—knowledge businesses and employee education. At the same time, six new R's from the business world will slowly seep into schools: an emphasis in the learning process on *risks, results, rewards, relationships, research,* and *rivalry.*

In their attempts to improve performance, some schools are consciously adopting practices that focus on these business values. Others will copy the successful school examples, not even aware that the origins of these practices are commercial. But in either case these developments have not occurred because the business community got together and asked, "How can we make schools more like us?"

In many instances, all parties have been unaware of these developments. In some they stem from public sector teachers and administrators seeing approaches that work in the private sector and realizing they would also find fertile soil in education. In others the influence comes more from the business community. However it happens, the shift from the public to the private sector in learning and education is already under way, and business approaches of all kinds will soon dominate the consumer and employee learning markets; they will also be internalized by students, teachers, and administrators in public education. The six R's are additional evidence that business, and its businesslike ways, are becoming the dominant educating institution in our society.

R#1   Risks

Businesses take risks and glorify risk takers. The value of risk is central to business mythology and business reality. The more entrepreneurial a company, the more risks it takes. Talented individuals, able to make bold decisions and pull off daring ideas, are praised in the press and heaped with adulation by all. Even entrepreneurs who fail are given second or more chances to "try, try again," until they succeed or bow out. Small companies that learn from failure and come back to win are more often the rule than the exception. The *Inc. 500* Entrepreneur of the Year Award is often given to those who have experienced failures prior to their success.

The pervasiveness of this value in business can also be seen in its reverse. Equally common are large companies that lose their capacity to learn from failure or are made arrogant by success. Risk aversion and overconfidence lead to decline and always top the list of faults in postmortems of the firms that fall off the *Fortune* 500 list. This is why there is so much talk in the business world about customer responsiveness, quality improvements, and the need for agile organizations. Yet very few large companies secure in their success are agile or responsive.

Arrogance is enemy number one to learning, whether in executives or teenagers. The less willing you are to take risks, the less able you are to learn. Where risk aversion and arrogance combine, dinosaurs are sure to be created. The education system today is one such dinosaur. Educational organizations are filled with risk-averse bureaucrats and administrators.

Monopoly is enemy number two of learning. Over the decades the schooling for ages five to eighteen became a monopoly and attracted large numbers of people who would perish in an entrepreneurial business environment. Laws that perpetuate marginal schools can run counter to their original purposes, just as child labor or minimum wage laws can have the unintended consequence of preventing young people from experiencing the world of work.

There are exceptions, of course. The 1983 Task Force that wrote "A Nation at Risk" was anything but risk averse. The teachers featured in popular films that portray a turnaround in an inner-city school take risks equal to those accepted by any entrepreneur. Studies by educational foundations, like Ford and Carnegie, have shown that individual principals are the most important element in school change, reform, and innovation. The history of American education is not lacking in great reformers who took risks, like Horace Mann, John Dewey, and Maria Montessori, to name a few. Theodore Sizer's "Re:learning" reform initiatives and John Goodlad's teacher effectiveness education are contemporary examples.

Such innovative risk-taking educators, however, are rarer than innovative risk takers in enterprise. As a necessary first step in educational reform, we need much more entrepreneurial risk taking at every level of the school system—teachers in classrooms, administrators in schools, school board members in communities, and authorities in state departments of education and in local, state, and federal education institutions.

There are many examples of risks that educational entrepreneurs might take in a business-influenced school system. At the high school level, one would be to integrate work and schooling. Many sophomores are not too young to work part-time. Work-study programs would apply to all students and be comparable to the way the ancient Greeks made physical and mental exercise equally important in their schools. The Walt Disney Company, for example, has an alliance with several local schools in Florida to integrate work and learning, although it applies not to students generally, but only to those who would otherwise be obliged to drop out of school.

The risk of incorporating work as an intrinsic part of the learning environment is that it is hard to monitor students when they leave the classroom and go off campus. Where it has been tried, cases are reported of students who "checked out" and went neither to work nor to school. In others, the work setting was beyond the students' skills, or they rapidly became bored by simple work. These mismatches occur because, systemically and historically in America, there is little synchronicity between work and school.

The case in Germany is quite different. There, an extensive apprenticeship system handles three-quarters of a million students learning at appropriate levels in 450 professions in over *half a million* companies.[1] Ninety-five percent of all apprentices are offered jobs in the companies where they trained. This is not to say that Germans have been more innovative in their schooling. Rather, they have developed an educational system over the course of five centuries that today is the envy of the rest of the world.

Hoechst, the large German chemical company, employs over six thousand apprentices at thirty-two manufacturing sites. The company's total cost amounts to 15 percent of annual net income, or DM 25,000 per apprentice, which is roughly the tuition at a private four-year college. Of the DM 25,000 about DM 13,000 are paid to the apprentice as salary. The total cost to German industry is DM 20 billion (U.S. $12 billion), or one-quarter of the total amount the German government spends on education.

We need risk taking now to adapt the German apprenticeship model and incorporate it into our system, which has never before married work and school. Such a program would have a greater chance of success from local entrepreneurs working with local community colleges than from government-sponsored programs that would involve huge costs, take forever to get started, and have as many administrators as students. "If one lesson can be learned from Germany," says Philip Glouchevitch, "it is that corporate America should take the initiative ahead of the politicians. Only then will apprenticeship programs be more of an asset than a cost."[2]

R#2 Results

Business is results oriented. In education, process counts at least as much as, if not more than, the results. As business becomes more involved in education, it will link rewards more and more to results for three groups—school administrators, teachers, and students.

The results-rewards equation in business should be most apparent for those at the top, but this is not always the case. There has recently been a tremendous outcry against CEOs who earned huge salaries regardless of their firm's performance. The picture is not always clear, however. A *BusinessWeek* cover story listed Roberto Goizueta, CEO of Coca Cola, as one executive who gave shareholders the least for their pay. *Fortune,* a month later, touted him on its cover for giving shareholders the most.[3] Salaries, however, are increasingly linked to performance. Measures such as executive compensation relative to shareholder return and to average return on equity are trends in this direction.

The picture is often no clearer in the world of education. Judging by the rapid turnover of college presidents and deans, the risks in these positions are surely great. The rewards of educational leaders should likewise be linked to the results they achieve, in terms of both the academic ranking and the fiscal solvency of their schools. Even though abuses of position will surface, this still should not invalidate the shift to rewards commensurate with results. John Silber of Boston University, for example, is the highest paid university president. He significantly raised the academic and fiscal standing of Boston University during his almost two decades as its "CEO." Many of his performance-based rewards, however, including corporate stocks and real estate, have come under justified scrutiny and moderate attack.

Ranking pay relative to performance is a business focus. Ranking pay at the top relative to pay at the bottom is a social focus. The multiple of a CEO's rewards package, compared with one of an average worker in the same company, is higher in the United States than in any other developed country. Ratios of ten to one and twenty to one are not uncommon. Ratios of five to one or six to one are more common in Japan and Europe, despite a variety of hidden rewards that do not show up, like million-dollar golf club memberships for Japanese executives.

At the teacher level in schools, merit increases are well intentioned but fail when they are applied within the education structure. They are a weak reed on which to hang educational reform. A typical scene is a group of teachers spending endless hours arguing about how to divide a department's paltry merit allotment. Ten people can spend ten hours in meetings dividing up $2,000. The discretionary range is far less in schools than in business, where the freedom to succeed also means the freedom to fail. No safety nets. DuPont, for example, recently cut its training staff by nearly half, not just to cut poor performers, but also to make room for new subjects.

A comparison of results among schools is as appropriate as a comparison of rewards relative to results among school leaders. Every year, for example, *BusinessWeek* ranks the nation's business schools. The measurements have become quite sophisticated, including rankings of judgments by students, deans, and employers' groups and also starting salaries for graduates by school. The rankings are widely known among school applicants, faculty, and prospective employers.

Because of these annual independent rankings, management schools examine themselves and their results in an ongoing dialogue that is similar to the planning, strategy, and competitive positioning meetings common to corporations. Colleges and universities do this to a lesser extent. They build up reputations that change only slowly over time and are seldom budged by facts because there is no systematic evaluation that is publicized.

Elementary and secondary schools are even further removed from the evaluation process. What if over time local high schools tracked the percent of their students who go to college, a weighted score for the quality of college a typical graduate attends, the percent who find employment, and so on? Even public schools would begin to define their market niches and the publics they serve. Parents could match their needs with what providers offer. Schools would do well to quantify and compare their results. Business would do well to extend this focus on results to more aspects of their own education activities.

Tuition reimbursement is a good case in point. Traditionally, it is treated as a benefit, and employees can take a wide variety of courses. Few companies tell their employees "Here are the subjects we most need people to be educated in." Companies should say they won't reimburse employees for taking courses where needs are nil or where there is greater supply than demand. How many say they will pay more than 100 percent for courses in areas where a shortage of skills has arisen? Companies should direct subsidies and rewards to where their needs will be and adjust the amounts on a sliding scale every six months until those needs are met. Business too often bemoans the shortage of trained people yet offers incentives to employees through tuition reimbursement programs to take courses that may not be relevant to its needs. Companies know their needs in the labor markets, and schools should follow their lead in directing students toward professions in demand.

Costs relative to results should be of equal concern to business and education. When the cost of business rises faster than the cost of inflation, companies have to respond quickly. Colleges do not. The cost of a four-year college education is now over $100,000 in many schools. Like spiraling health care costs, tuition is expanding at two and three times the inflation rate and cannot go on like this indefinitely.

Business's concern with results also manifests itself in time-based competition. It focuses first on a desired result and then competes for how quickly it can be achieved. Europe and Detroit can move a new car from concept to customer in thirty-six months; Toyota can do it in twenty-some months and is shooting for eighteen. Distribution is a major portion of the cost of a car. It takes Detroit about six weeks to deliver a special-order car, but Toyota can do it in one week. Ford and other United States auto makers have invested a lot of psychological and financial capital to catch up.

Schools will have to take similar steps. Students, as a kind of work in process, for example, are measured not by results, but by "time spent," as in prison. You get out only after a certain number of years, the school year has 180 days, course credits are awarded after a certain number of hours, and classes are fifty minutes. This is a time-based system that is not linked to results.

Grades are another measure of students' results that differ greatly from the current business approach to evaluation. Teachers typically give grades like old-time production line inspectors, according to percentages along a normal curve: ten A's, twenty B's, forty C's, twenty D's, and ten F's. This system may serve well in deciding who will or will not go to college. But no business (or government, for that matter) wants to hire 10 percent failures and 20 percent near failures in the hope of getting a few successes. That's why less than 15 percent of prospective employers look at an applicant's grades. Grade inflation, where almost everyone gets an A or B, corrupts the measure further to where it should be all but thrown out. When parents pay close to $100,000 for their child's education in a private four-year university, it is shrewd for that university to graduate 40 percent of its students cum laude or better.

When you go to the bank for a loan to pay that tuition bill, you want your application handled by someone who is knowledgeable and competent about finances, not someone who failed to master basic mathematics. This same dynamic applies to all functions in the knowledge economy. Whether it's hamburger flipping or medical research, we want to transact business with people who are competent to do their job, not with people who have failed to learn their trade. In a business-driven model, the normal curve would be dropped in favor of certificates of mastery, or competency-based education.

Many businesses use formal feedback techniques to get desired results in their managerial development courses. Nearly every corporate seminar or workshop, whether one day or one month, ends with an evaluation of the instructor's performance. Did the seminar meet your needs? Was the instructor well prepared? Can you use what you learned back on your job? What are your suggestions for improvement? These are questions routinely asked in corporate education settings that are nearly unthinkable in public schools. This emphasis on customer service, in the case of students, would greatly benefit schools.

DuPont, for example, uses what is called a "360-degree feedback" method. When employees finish a training course, instead of grades they learn how their bosses, peers, and subordinates evaluate their progress and in what areas they need improvement. Then they go to work to reach acceptable levels. Some schools evaluate students this way, but they are the exception. In Vermont students keep samples and records of their work in portfolios, much as photographers keep portfolios of their best pictures, from which their progress is evaluated. This system is also used in some San Francisco high schools.

R#3 Rewards

Rewards will increasingly work their way into a business-influenced education system with dramatic effects. People who work in education generally rank job security as a greater reward than pay. Business reverses the order, making pay the most important reward and increasingly linking it to R#2, results.

Unions, particularly teachers unions, generally emphasize job security over pay and resist performance-based rewards. In education the influence of business is climbing, while that of unions is declining, and the size and ranking of rewards will shift accordingly. Pay will increasingly be tied to performance, and job security will disappear. The process may take a generation, but signs of trends in this direction are already evident.

Tenure is the Cadillac of academic job security, put in place to protect academic freedom and to prevent teachers from being fired for political reasons. It will be challenged and ultimately abandoned for many of the same reasons that business resists seniority systems—such as the unfortunate fact that both tenure and seniority end up protecting incompetence. Harvard Medical School graduate and popular novelist Michael Crichton put it well when he said, "There is no such thing as a free market. Haven't you noticed how many free market advocates want tenure?" The old paradox is true. Those who deserve tenure don't need it, and those who need it don't deserve it.

Business, too, had its own forms of tenure. IBM was the most famous American company with tenure, called "no layoffs," until the giant's recent fall and the release—both "voluntarily" and not—of one hundred thousand "lifetime" employees. Tenure is called lifetime employment in Japan. It was introduced by Toyota in 1953 and was sacred throughout the country until only a few years ago, when criticism of the disguised forms of underemployment came under attack. Today Japanese companies will, and do, lay off personnel.

In the industrial economy unions were the major force for protecting workers' job security, but in an information economy knowledge workers own both the means and the tools of production, and unions are rapidly becoming a thing of the past. Union membership has dropped from 35 percent of the labor force in 1954 to 16 percent in 1989. Industrial unions won job security for workers, only to find that it was meaningless if their output was noncompetitive and their companies closed. Teachers unions will find the same thing. The pendulum swung too far in both academia and the business world. It is swinging back now in business and will soon do the same in education. Teachers who unionize define themselves as workers, not managers, and concede rather than delegate the running of the school to administrators. Decentralization and the empowerment of local teachers and administrators are healthier steps than unionization.

There are more creative ways than tenure to protect educational job security. One is a rolling contract. Once teachers reach a certain level of competence, they can be placed on a three-year rolling contract. At the end of a year, the contract rolls over automatically, and they still have a blanket of protection three years into the future. If the administration chooses not to roll it over, then the individual has two years of job security and an appeals process may kick in automatically. This is less than tenured academics expect, but more than the private sector awards to most nonperforming members.

Kentucky has proposed another creative approach, this one tied to performance. As part of its 1990 school reform legislation, individual schools are accountable for improving student performance on standard measurements. If the school fails to achieve results within two years, tenure may be lifted and teachers may be fired regardless of prior guarantees. The results are not yet apparent, and it is not clear whether the approach is rhetorical or real.

There is, of course, more to rewards than job security. Low salaries are a common complaint. Average teachers' income in 1992–1993 was $35,334 for about a nine-month school year. Yet this is substantially higher than the 1992 *twelve*-month median household income of $30,786. Administrators, on average, earn slightly more than teachers. High school principals, for example, earn about 50 percent more than their teachers. These amounts are far from generous for such an important profession, and industry counterparts who train employees and teach executives earn double these figures.

The pay gap between teachers in school and trainers in business is unlikely to narrow very much. What we can expect, however, is more teaching jobs at higher pay in business. AT&T Bell Labs, for example, regularly hires public school teachers to moderate experiments and focus groups in its consumer research labs. We can also expect a tighter linkage among security, pay, and performance for educators in the public sector. This is what Ross Perot's commission did in the Texas school system, where teachers now have to be certified by periodic standardized tests to keep their jobs. We would benefit by extending this concept to teachers and education administrators nationwide.

Even better than certification renewals, however, would be for the marketplace to play a role in judging performance. Student evaluations of courses and teachers became commonplace in private colleges and universities during the past two decades. They are less common in public centers of higher education yet would be a great benefit. They are the equivalent of customer feedback in the private sector and would link risks and results to rewards.

R#4   Relationships

There are over 140,000 explicit school-business relationships.[4] Nearly half the schools in the United States have some sort of alliance with a business corporation. The most meaningful alliances are in research. As of the early 1990s, about 90 percent of business funding to education was targeted at the university level. The lion's share of the more than $6 billion given annually went to the top forty research universities. Some individual grants are as large as $150 million.

The bulk of the school-business relationships in the K–12 sector involves teaching and support of special programs, such as loan-a-teacher arrangements or adopt-a-school programs. The Walt Disney Company has more than a dozen different alliances with local Florida schools and teachers. Through its *Challenge Program,* forty-two high school students at risk of dropping out are offered a way to stay in school. The *Teacher-rific Merit Awards* give outstanding teachers $1,000 awards in 180 Florida public schools. In New England, Digital Equipment sponsors a $7 million "Engineers in Education" program, which provides good math and science teachers to schools that need them. AT&T adopts local schools in New Jersey, General Motors sponsors school programs in Detroit, Chevron gives support in San Francisco. IBM supports over one hundred schools in local communities across the country. All of these are honorable gestures but have little or no impact on the fifteen thousand or so school districts across the country. These major corporate players could spend their money with greater leverage and effectiveness.

Self-interest is the main reason business enters into alliances with schools. Sometimes the motivation is to head off an impending shortage of qualified labor, as with the job-on-graduation promises made by a group of businesses in the Boston Compact. Other times the goal is to introduce the company's technology products to students, as when Apple distributed its computers in the classroom. Corporations also get involved for public relations, to be good corporate citizens. RJR Nabisco, for example, makes grants to forty-five schools in its Next Century Schools program.

The variety of alliances is astounding. Sara Lee supports arts programs for high schools in Winston-Salem on the theory that creativity in the arts can lead to creativity in inventing new products. The lumber company Georgia Pacific funds teachers in Glynn County schools in Brunswick, Georgia, to teach computer modeling and simulation to elementary students as a new way of thinking developed at MIT. Its support allows even kindergarteners to be counseled by High Performance Systems, Inc., a $2 million software firm in Hanover, New Hampshire.

Japanese companies, or their American branches, have partnerships with American schools. Panasonic, through its corporate foundation, supports nine different high schools across the nation. Mitsubishi created a stir when it made a major contribution to MIT to support a Japanese studies program. German and Swiss pharmaceutical firms likewise raised eyebrows when they contributed to American schools.

One of the largest efforts to encourage business to support schools is NASDC, the New American Schools Development Corporation, launched by the Bush administration and supported by the Clinton administration. It has collected about half of its $200 million goal and has nine design teams working in more than 150 schools.

While K–12 teaching alliances dominate numerically, the majority of them patch up what doesn't work or depend on companies to make up for shortfalls created by government cutbacks. They are largely ameliorative and seldom redefine local level learning, let alone the entire education system. To be most effective, these alliances have to be more than just public relations; they must redefine and restructure the way things are done. Relationships that have a clear and explicit business objective have a better chance of succeeding and of redefining the learning process in schools. The high-powered group in the *Fortune* Education Summit has begun to stress strategy over philanthropy. CEO members from companies like Boeing, Hewlett-Packard, and Pacific Telesis are working to make this shift.

Many educators are concerned that these relationships, partnerships, and alliances between commerce and learning will compromise academic freedom and skew research toward science and technology at the expense of the arts and humanities. For decades there were fierce debates about these issues. Most of the protests about academic freedom have withered away, and now the irony is that government is cutting school budgets for music, arts, and sports while business picks up the slack.

Many relationships between schools and businesses focus on learning, and some are redefining educational roles. An intriguing example occurs when companies arrange for employees to earn university credits for company training. AT&T directly teaches seventy-five courses that carry academic credit to employees. Ford delivers for-credit courses at fifty sites in partnership with the

United Auto Workers union, through the UAW/Ford National Education, Development, and Training Center. The University of Kentucky's state system willingly approves corporate-generated credits. "If I grant people who are trained on laser drilling machines six credits toward a laser optics degree," says the university's coordinator of business and industry services, "I have a better chance of getting them to sign on for a degree." Business training for academic credit benefits both companies and employees, and universities gain by being able to broaden their course offerings without having to increase their staff or facilities.

How common are programs like these? The American Council on Education (ACE) is a nonprofit educational lobby in Washington that has been evaluating the creditworthiness of corporate courses since 1974. In 1990, for the first time, ACE had a waiting list of companies that wanted evaluation teams. The teams, made up of faculty from different universities, attend classes, review curricula and materials, judge grading practices, and ensure that the learning is not company specific. Independent, for-profit education companies, such as Dale Carnegie & Associates, and not-for-profit organizations, such as the Conference Board, have also gotten college accreditation for many of their offerings.

In an evolution that is viewed as mutually beneficial, corporations are helping schools while intentionally steering clear of any regulatory role. They let impartial third parties such as ACE decide which courses merit college credit. At the same time, the universities are letting the corporations determine which courses they should offer and what should be taught in them, resulting in a more direct, relevant relationship between campus and corporation.

Another type of educational relationship, the voluntary corporate program, has also become a big draw. The Conference Board polled 454 human resources, community relations, and public affairs executives about their businesses and found that voluntary employee programs in education far outnumbered other programs: 74 percent of those polled had some kind of voluntary employee program in education, whereas only 47 percent had programs in either health or youths in crisis, and a scant 41 percent had programs in either the environment or homelessness.

Media companies are, of course, interested in the school market. Television is now in the classroom thanks to Channel 1. A consortium of film companies in Los Angeles called Education First! gives funds to support critical analysis of media. National Media Literacy, chaired by *20/20* host Hugh Downs, is working to include media literacy in high school curricula.

The Wall Street Journal publishes a special classroom edition and advertises it as "how to improve America's future, one classroom at a time." For $150, a person or a company can adopt a class, entitling it to receive thirty copies of *TWSJ* classroom edition throughout the school year. For another $60 per semester, *TWSJ* will include four videos "to enhance the learning experience." Adopt more than fifty classrooms, and *TWSJ* will provide sponsored teachers with a training workshop. The newspaper gets more than public relations value from this program, which is probably more likely to survive recessions than are other purely philanthropic arrangements.

Business's concept of teamwork is also gaining currency in the school world. When businesses seek to solve a problem, they often create a task force or team because of a deeply held belief that combining varying perspectives helps to solve complex problems. By contrast, educators historically have insisted that students solve problems for themselves. Team learning is still often considered cheating, even though team teaching is acceptable. Only during the last decade have educators realized that cooperation in the classroom yields results superior to those achieved through competition among students.

## R#5	Research

Many school-business relationships focus on products and processes more than on teaching. This type of relationship exists chiefly in research universities. Creation of new knowledge through research is concentrated in university labs like MIT (large), federal defense labs like Los Alamos (larger), and business labs like AT&T Bell Laboratories (largest). Universities account for about 60 percent of all basic research, and government and corporate labs share the remainder. Universities traditionally operated on a "publish or perish" principle, defense labs on "protect or perish," and commercial labs on "patent or perish." Now all three are converging, and their relationships are changing. Through liaison programs and partnerships, academia is becoming more interested in applications, defense labs are converting to civilian uses, and business is getting involved in longer-term projects.

In the industrial era, the pace of change was still relatively slow; basic research could remain separate from applied research, and universities could concentrate on the former and business and the military on the latter. New knowledge emanating from inventors or universities could be transformed into useful products within a time frame that met public demands. The steam engine, for example, was invented in the mid-1800s and adapted for use by railroads fifty years later. Alexander Graham Bell invented the telephone at Boston University in 1876; telephone service began in earnest twenty-five years later.

In the information era, however, the time lapse between basic and applied research is compressed. Transistors were invented in 1954 and were used in integrated circuits to produce computers within five years. Discoveries in superconductivity at the University of Houston and IBM's Laboratories in Zurich in 1985 created entire new industries within three years. There are now powerful pressures to shorten the time span between basic research and its application, resulting in a burgeoning of alliances between businesses and universities. In the process, business practices in research are seeping into the university, and vice versa.

Generally, these alliances take the form of a consortium led by a single university and joined by one or more companies, often with matching state or federal government funding. Most of these alliances seek to leverage universities' basic research efforts with business's agenda for application. Early critics of such arrangements asserted that business would corrupt the search for new knowledge, but to date the benefits far outweigh the costs. Several hundred such alliances have been created since the National Cooperative Research Act was passed in 1984, allowing competitors to join with one another without fear of violating antitrust laws. Probably no single *Fortune* 500 company is not a member of at least one such research alliance with a university.

Examples are plentiful. Stanford University sponsors the Center for Integrated Systems, whose purpose is research on semiconductor design and fabrication. Nine leading corporations are members: GE, Intel, Apple, National Semiconductor, Philips, Texas Instruments, IBM, HP, and Motorola. All nine have as their goal the discovery and development of a better process for wafer fabrication. A secondary goal is to train graduate students who might then become new hires. Since its founding in 1980, more than $25 million has been invested in the center's research.

Rochester University in New York State runs a similar center, the Center for Advanced Optical Technology (Rochester and the University of Arizona are the two leading centers in the United States for optics). Kodak and Xerox are two of its six major supporters. Rutgers University has the Center for Ceramics Research. Purdue has the Computer Integrated Design, Manufacturing, and Automation Center. Rensselaer Polytechnic has the Center for Industrial Innovation, one of the largest alliances in the country, with more than two hundred participating companies. Carnegie Mellon University has a Robotics Institute. North Carolina has a Microelectronics Center, which includes a consortium of six universities in addition to many businesses.

AT&T's "corporate partnership" with Indiana University's Center for Excellence in Education has built a classroom of the future that incorporates the latest telecommunications technologies. AT&T gets to showcase its equipment and brings specific problems to the university for solution. Relations like these are based on the notion that various university players have different skills from those of people in enterprise and that each part of a task should be assigned to those most skilled at it.

The pattern of research alliance between business and education is expanding beyond information age technologies and involving similar research efforts in biotechnology, new materials, energy, and space research. Today's young computer science professor is as likely to be tied into IBM or Apple as into the University of California. The same holds true, with different companies, for the assistant professor in biology or materials engineering.

Federal and state governments provide little in the way of funds to improve learning and teaching. Nationally, less than .1 percent of our school budgets is destined for educational research—the lowest figure for research spent on any major budgeted activity. Compared with health, defense, technology, space, energy, or new products, new knowledge on the learning process is definitely a poor relation. The $350 million that government spends on educational research is less than .5 percent of all government research funds allocated in 1991. The federal government spends three times more for agricultural research, twenty-one times more for space research, and thirty times more for research in health.[5] We know more about how to improve the use of diapers than of brains.

The private sector has stepped in to pick up the slack. In 1987, for example, David Kearns, then chairman and CEO of Xerox, founded the Institute for Research on Learning (IRL) with an initial five-year, $5 million commitment. The institute is located close to Xerox PARC in California and is headed by Peter Henschel, a former deputy mayor of San Francisco. A dozen companies, in addition to Xerox, now work in concert to support it. Its results are being adopted by many companies and several participating schools.[6]

"Education," according to Robert Frost, "is hanging around until you've caught on." The work of IRL shows that learning is fundamentally social, what they call "communities of practice." This interactive concept is in stark contrast with the more traditional view that learning is a one-way street from teacher to student and from trainer to employee. Further, the choice we face between work and school is one that should never arise, and reintegrating learning and work is a major IRL priority. A further example of business-supported research on learning is Arthur Andersen's partnership with the Institute for the Learning Sciences at Northwestern University.

Few significant business-university research alliances focus on literature, fine arts, theater, or music. As information technologies transform the way literature is written and distributed, and the manner in which music is created and performed, such alliances will surely emerge.

Business plays an even greater role in research in Japan than it does in the United States. Few major Japanese universities conduct extensive research. When the famous Fifth Generation computer project was started in 1986, the University of Tokyo played a central role, not in conducting research, but in playing referee among Hitachi, Toshiba, NEC Corporation, and the five other Japanese partners with strong research orientations. The project was a failure nevertheless.

Germany has the oldest tradition of universities devoted primarily or exclusively to research. The Technical University of Berlin and the old Alexander Humboldt University are well-known examples. America, too, has true research universities. Johns Hopkins University in Maryland and Rockefeller University in New York, for example, are modeled after their German predecessors, and both have increasing alliances with business. As in the United States, business in Germany is beginning to play a more active role in the support and influence of German research universities.

The role of business in university research, however, is not increasing at the same rate everywhere. In France, with its centralized Ministry of Education, business influence has been slow to develop because the government still plays the dominant role. In Spain the Catholic Church is still more influential than the business community. In the former Soviet Union, until recently, the military and the central government were dominant. Now emerging Russian and Ukrainian businesses are beginning to appear in traditional university institutes.

Wherever the pressures of the information age are felt, business is playing a greater role in university research. Although mitigated in different countries by the history and strength of other institutions such as church, government, and military, alliances between business and education are on the rise around the world.

R#6   Rivalry

Rivalry, or competition, is one of the most basic business practices having an impact on education. In free market economies, business by definition has been built on competition. Deregulation, privatization, and the demise of communism further confirm the benefits of competition. Even in the health care field, where competition is most ill at ease, reform movements aim at "managed competition." Making institutions more responsive to those they serve is clearly an idea of sweeping popularity. Why not for schools?

Rivalry is nothing new to schools in sports, debating, accomplishments of graduates, reputation, and other areas. Private and parochial schools regularly compete with one another; indirectly they compete with public schools. Some public universities, such as UC Berkeley, surpass their private counterparts, top the popularity list, and vie actively for the best students.

Some public grammar schools are trying to become competitive by contracting out their activities. Education Alternatives, Inc. (EAI), is a Minneapolis-based, for-profit company set up to manage public schools. In partnership with Johnson Controls, which specializes in maintenance services, and KPMG Peat Marwick, EAI is running schools in Miami, Baltimore, Duluth, and St. Paul. The Baltimore contract, signed in 1992, is to run nine schools for five years at $27 million a year.

EAI stock grew 56 percent in the first half of 1993, two years after going public, and the company reported a net income for the first time. Seventy percent of its stock is owned by large institutions, which is unusually high for a startup and helps stability. Despite this, EAI stock fluctuates wildly when newspaper headlines announce a new development. In December of 1993, for example, it went down 10 percent when the Baltimore Teachers Union filed suit challenging the EAI contract. Then it went up almost as much a week later when the Baltimore Board of Estimates approved EAI contracts at two additional schools and the Washington, D.C., school system expressed interest in EAI.

EAI's approach is to run schools as public utilities, with private management as the contracted agent of public regulators—the school board. Its goal is to reinvent, not circumvent public school systems. Private management of public services sounds like a bright idea, but it hasn't caught on. EAI's management would like to see competition, because it validates their concept, but they think the likelihood is low because of the need for capital, time, and credibility. The Edison Project is one such competitor.

Vouchers are another example of competition in the public school arena. Unlike the other R's, which are seeping quietly into schools by osmosis, rivalry in the form of vouchers, or school choice, has excited controversy in the megadecibels. The pros and cons of choice have been highly politicized and exaggerated to an extreme. California, Colorado, and Michigan put proposals for vouchers on their ballots, and twelve additional states voted on tax aid to parochial schools. The idea is that funds collected through property taxes would be converted into vouchers, instead of being allocated directly to schools. These vouchers would be divided up among parents according to the number of school-age children they have, and they could then choose the school they thought best for their child. The logic is that over time, the better the school, the more voucher funds it will receive, thus transforming the system from a regulated monopoly to free-market competition.

This process is hauntingly similar to the one instituted in former socialist countries to make their industries more competitive: there, vouchers were issued to privatize formerly state-owned enterprises. As Poland, Russia, and other countries have discovered, such a basic shift is a monumental task. The same will surely be true in education in America. Like other business practices, competition in schools holds many benefits, but whether it can be mandated by government action or voting is questionable. To really get into schools, competition will probably have to occur silently and in small steps, again like other business practices.

Not content to wait for political action, some businesses have funded private choice programs. Privately funded school-choice programs have been launched in Indianapolis, Atlanta, Milwaukee, San Antonio, Little Rock, and Prince Georges County, Maryland. Grants from groups like the Free to Choose Trust average about $1,000 per parent and are funded by local business leaders.

Like most new initiatives that challenge established practices, the voucher and choice system carries with it several easily identifiable risks and problems. Many laws regulating public schools would have to be modified. The 1975 Education for All Handicapped Children Act, for example, requires public but not private schools to accept handicapped children. This is a substantial burden for public competitors, since there are nearly four million such children of elementary and secondary school age whose schooling can cost $40,000–$50,000 per year per child. Likewise, bilingual education is required for public schools but not for private ones. And public school systems maintain fleets of buses, while private schools do not. It's not that objections like these cannot be overcome, it's that they illustrate the myriad details that would have to be worked out in order to make a voucher system operable.

The greatest objection is that a voucher system would make the wealthy schools even wealthier and the poor schools responsible for the least able students. This is a variation on the objection to tax codes—that the wealthy know how to take advantage of them while the poor do not. Choice and vouchers, nevertheless, have worked for years in schools in New York City's Harlem.

School choice and vouchers would be less needed if schools were funded nationally, with an equal amount being given to each. While this is impossible politically because of our decentralized traditions, it should be possible at the state level. If every school in a state was funded equally, we might shuttle children around less to get them to the better schools. To be sure, there would still be good and bad schools, but the quality of education would be less linked to factors other than race and wealth.

There is strong support for the notion that competition in the school system will lead to much needed improvements in education, but great skepticism that voucher programs administered by local, state, and federal governments will result in the intended effect. Usually, where such plans are tried, those with access to the most information and knowledge will benefit while those already in an educational underclass will not. This will only intensify social frictions at a time when the use of schools to implement social justice rather than learning will be increasingly challenged. Had voucher programs been tried during an industrial economy when capital was the key resource, they might have succeeded. But to institute a voucher system in an economy in which knowledge is the key resource will offer too little too late and is bound to produce unintended side effects. Yet without doubt, competition, like other business practices, is already finding its way into all levels of education.

CHAPTER 7

FOR BETTER AND FOR WORSE

If I am not for myself, who will be for me?
If I am only for myself, who am I?
If not now, when?

—HILLEL, first century

"Wilt thou take this person for better and for worse . . ." Anything as meaningful and important as marriage is not likely to be all for the better or totally for the worse or a consistent blend somewhere in between. There will be both good times and bad times. Major changes in our lives as well as in our society also have this effect, making things better in some ways and worse in others, and seemingly both at once. So it is with the ways that learning will revolutionize business and the ways that business will revolutionize learning. The decline of a government-led school system, the rise of business-led ways of educating, the revolutionary shift to lifelong learning, and the growth of knowledge-based businesses—all will produce changes that are for better *and* for worse.

BEWARE THE TWO-TIER SOCIETY

Industrialization made the United States the richest nation on earth, yet we also have the greatest income disparity, internally, of any developed nation. Ten percent of the United States population controls 90 percent of the wealth. Taxation, as a government method to redistribute income, has not eliminated these inequalities.

Similarly, of every nation in the world, a greater percent of our population undertakes higher education. While not number one by every measure, we spend a greater percent of our GNP on education than almost any other nation, the percentage of young people in college is double that of Great Britain, and we have the largest learning sector of any developed nation. At the same time, we have some of the worst illiteracy rates of any developed country, an alarming dropout rate from high schools, and a widening spread between the highest achievers and the lowest.

And money is not the entire issue. The ten states that spent the most per pupil were all in the bottom two-fifths on Scholastic Aptitude Test rankings, and nine of the ten states that spent the least were in the top two-fifths. Minnesota, the state whose average per-pupil expenditure was virtually identical with the national average ($5,261), was third in the SAT rankings. Iowa, North Dakota, and Minnesota ranked as the top three states in National Association of Educational Progress (NAEP) eighth-grade math test scores yet ranked only twenty-seven, forty-four, and twenty-five respectively in per-pupil expenditure in 1992–1993.

Such statistics do not, however, support the notion that spending doesn't count in education. All these states also have very few students from minorities, from homes that do not speak English, or from families living below the poverty line. New Jersey and Connecticut ranked first and third in 1992–1993 pupil expenditure and a very respectable fourteen and eleven in NAEP eighth-grade math test scores, despite the challenge of 35 and 25 percent minority enrollments. Neither money spent nor cultural diversity, by themselves, explain gaps in educational performance. Nevertheless the disparities persist.

We are, as some outside America like to say, the best schooled and least educated. Or, in short, we are both the smartest and the dumbest. These disparities occurred on government's watch, when it dominated the education system, yet the government has been unable to reverse the disparities in knowledge any more than in income. This is so, despite the fact that government has made educational equality a national priority. Head Start programs, mandated bilingual education where needed, busing initiatives to integrate poorer and racially segregated pupils into richer schools: these are examples of government's efforts to reverse the slide toward a permanent uneducated underclass. But the gap between those who know and those who don't continues to grow.

The high school dropout rate, despite marginal improvement, remains at around 30 percent, approaching 50 percent in inner cities. The claim made by some studies that a quarter of graduating students are barely able to read their own diplomas may be exaggerated—but not by much. Americans routinely score at the bottom of the list of OECD (Organization for Economic Cooperation and Development) country students in math, science, language, and other subjects.

Only part of the need for remediation can be traced to faults in the public schools. Some is also due to the rapid pace of change and the inevitable obsolescence of knowledge gained while young. Even a perfect public school system is not guaranteed protection from the need for remediation.

Will business be any more successful than government in narrowing the knowledge gap? Should this be its role? Schooling was never the primary role of either government or business, even though the former assumed responsibility for it long ago and the latter is taking it on now. In both cases this occurred, at least in part, without clear intention and sometimes without even conscious awareness until after the fact.

The role of business as educator demands—and is dependent upon—recognizing the enormous profit potential of the business of knowledge and viewing employees and consumers as learners. At this point, before it gets too deeply into the process, business would do well to be clear about its primary purpose and how its purpose differs substantially from that of a school system.

Business's primary purpose is to meet market needs with its production and distribution of goods and services. But as it increasingly produces and distributes knowledge in carrying out this function, it must also accept the social responsibility incumbent upon an educator. Business should be acknowledged, for example, for its part in extending learning to new, lifelong segments. It should also be cautioned against prolonging a failed educational system with misguided, albeit well-intentioned, philanthropy.

Business is as concerned about the unproductive, unhirable, and unreachable underclass as is government and as are the average citizens of the "overclass." But in creating an information economy, given the increased importance and value of knowledge and knowledge workers, it cannot be blamed for also creating the underclass—and eliminating it is not its principal task.

A school system's primary purpose is to educate and prepare people for society. This socializing role is especially important for homogenizing an ethnically diverse population. Yet socialization must be balanced with economic relevancy for both individual livelihood and national vigor. Education has to prepare people to hold jobs, specifically the kinds of jobs that a learning and knowledge society creates. Schools should be acknowledged for addressing social problems, and they should be commended for focusing on the forgotten. But they should also realize that they are now specialized niche educators, with only a portion of the learning market, and should focus on their primary purpose, not broaden it.

Learning should never be the principal duty of business, any more than social justice should be the primary function of the education system. Each benefits from pluralism, but neither should sacrifice its major objective in the process.

Business is slowly awakening to its new role and taking some responsibility for dealing with the growing disparities in levels of education. Remedial education in the workplace, while accorded only about 10 percent of corporate funding for training, is a necessity that has gained the grudging support of most companies.

Business also has considerable experience in training for diversity. "Workforce 2000," issued by the Hudson Institute in 1987, said that by the turn of the century, 85 percent of new hires would be minorities and females. Ever since, nearly every company has instituted employee education on how to leverage and take advantage of this demographic diversity in its marketing, its culture, and its employees. Some might complain that the response is inadequate, but the program did not have to be legally mandated. In government-run schools, programs to achieve diversity, like busing, are driven by legislation, not demographic forecasts. Diversity programs in business are driven by self-interest, not self-sacrifice.

Since business will look first to its self-interest, it will concentrate on knowledge businesses and employee education; only reluctantly will it undertake conventional public schooling. What will happen to the public schools? Will they increasingly become the repository of the underclass? Metal detectors in schools confront teachers and administrators with the struggle between freedom and order. Vouchers for school choice force us to choose between competence and cohesion. The transition from government-led to business-led learning highlights these trade-offs, which are painful reminders that public schools are the dumping ground for many of society's ills. Still, business may become the major educating institution addressing our social problems, for better and for worse, and during its tenure may fail to alter the situation we face today. It's also possible that the situation will worsen, creating a two-tier society of haves and have-nots, voters and vote-nots, knowers and know-nots. We are in danger of imprisoning nearly half our population in a permanent underclass.

The Wall Street Journal reports that as many as twenty-five million jobs, over a quarter of the employment in the private sector, may be wiped out in the reorganization of work during the next decade—that is, in the knowledge stage of the information economy. This will produce a social transformation as radical and traumatic as the one that occurred during the Industrial Revolution. Indeed, the sea shift in who educates whom, how, and for what is a by-product and a reflection of this larger drama.

The previous economy suffered a comparable workforce contraction; today the U.S. economy produces five times as many goods as it did at the end of World War II, with about the same number of production workers. The last time around, however, workers expelled from the gain in productivity found new jobs in services. This time jobs in new sectors may be reserved for knowledgeable workers of the coming generation, leaving the unemployed with nowhere to go.

Those left after the cutbacks are presumably the best of the crop. So the smart get smarter. Knowledge workers, not minimum wage workers, represent the maturation of service organizations. Their jobs broaden in scope and responsibility. Companies that define their strategies around knowledge, evaluate their human assets as more valuable than brick and mortar, but only inch their way toward investing in human development are destined to perpetuate the status quo.

Charles Handy, author of *The Age of Unreason,* believes that the dimensions of many companies will change by "½ × 2 × 3" over the next five years. That is, they will have half as many people, pay them twice as much, and produce three times as much value. The first number reflects the mass exodus resulting from the downsizing of corporate America. The second number addresses the increased concentration of knowledge workers, who will presumably command better salaries. The third speaks to a goal of multiple increases in productivity.

Downsizing, employing knowledge workers, and increasing productivity are three distinct trends that will have major social consequences. By itself, downsizing serves only to clean up past mistakes, clearing away the bloat in companies overcomplacent with past success. If this can be done without loss of productivity, then the corporate body will truly be better off. But tripling productivity requires some genius, and such smart workers will want their rewards. This isn't Reagan-era trickle-down economics, but it does create greater income inequality and a larger gap between the top and the bottom of the social pyramid.

Either way, this is a dark side and a downside of the learning revolution that we must guard against. The spread of learning and education throughout the marketplace, by business or by government, does not necessarily mean a better life for those at the bottom. In fact, we may find an even larger gap between those who know how to use knowledge and those who don't. Technology is pushing us to value knowledge, but only society can push us to lesser or greater equality in the distribution of knowledge products and services.

Basic education is essential for a person to earn a living and for a nation to sustain growth. Beyond that, lifelong learning is essential if the person and nation are to rise and stay at the top. The exclusion of business from school-based learning, and of government from lifelong learning, is impractical and unrealistic.

To maximize the better and minimize the worse, basic education should not be a monopoly of government, any more than lifelong learning should be a monopoly of business. Each should play dominant roles in one segment and active minor roles in the other. Strict separation of educating roles would hasten the division of society into two tiers. It would create an equality of losers and a meritocracy of winners. It would almost guarantee the growth of both an underclass and an elite, with no understanding or mobility between them. The energy, freedom, and pluralism unleashed by the learning revolution must act as bridges to link society's classes, not wedges that split them apart.

Can We Balance Prosperity and Freedom?

A nation's great internal struggle is often its attempt to balance economic performance with social and political cohesion. Disaster generally accompanies too much success in one area at the expense of the other. If one gets better while the other stagnates or deteriorates, ultimately both are drawn down. However, acceptable differences lie in which arm leads and in how closely the dragging arm keeps up. Here, too, we need balance and bridges.

In the former Soviet Union, glasnost (openness) got way ahead of perestroika (restructuring), and the republics that have now emerged are suffering a series of economic breakdowns that threaten their fragile democracies. After the Tiananmen Square repression, China chose to favor economic growth over freedom, reaching an astounding 18 percent growth rate in the southern coastal regions. Political pressures will build again when Britain returns Hong Kong to China.

Germany also has had to balance social and political unification with the economic integration of its former eastern and western halves. Chancellor Helmut Kohl chose the former, at the expense of a severe financial crisis. The same syncopations are evident in developing countries like India, Korea, Mexico, and Chile. Ethnic tribalism and/or religious fundamentalism are symptoms of current imbalances among these social, political, and economic forces, in both developed and developing countries.

Americans are pleased to see the rise of market economies in Eastern Europe, while at the same time we worry about the social dislocations the shift is causing. It does not seem to matter whether these market economies offer industrial rather than information infrastructures. Cellular phones are leapfrogging poorly wired telephone systems in Eastern Europe, for example, yet we don't seem concerned that only knowledge workers will have them while the majority of the population will wait years even for rudimentary telephone service.

In other words, we applaud market economies whatever their infrastructure. We prefer them because, on balance, they are more neutral than command economies and because they facilitate the achievement of a better life for a larger number. Is this any less true in Western Europe and the United States? Of course not.

The United States also struggles with the fragile balance among these forces. On the one hand, our economic growth rate is rather poor, yet we have significant political freedoms. On the other hand, we are the richest nation on earth, yet we incarcerate and also execute more people per capita than any other developed nation. Videotaped police beatings led to the worst rioting in the country's history. Hundreds of millions of dollars from Japanese and European tourism to the United States is threatened because of violence to foreign visitors. More Japanese are murdered in the United States, per capita, than in Japan.

There will always be some tension between social and economic needs. Meeting both are necessary; they are not alternatives to choose between. The same can be said for freedom and order. Freedom springs from intuition and leads to innovation. Order stems from intelligence and provides efficiency. Both are essential, but are they compatible? At every given moment we must choose which needs a little nudge to maintain the best possible balance.

Compassion versus competitiveness is a position of false opposites. Economies must stay competitive so that they have the means to be compassionate. Loss of competitiveness hardly increases compassion. Whether or not people choose to be compassionate is not related to any given level of technology. Compassion, whether in the form of fairer income distribution, equal access to education, or a pollution-free environment, is the result of social and political choices. These rest on an economic base that is driven by technology, and a more developed base gives us more resources to work with. How we use them is up to us more than it is up to the technologies employed.

Neither Pollyannas nor doomsayers will have the last word on the consequences as learning and business revolutionize each other. We must see both the good and the bad, and choosing to focus on the potential for good does not mean we are blind to the bad.

Opposites are not contradictions; they need each other to exist. As in any good marriage, success comes from valuing the traits of each other—even while they irritate—because of a greater shared belief that the contribution of both parties is necessary to make things work. We seek these creative tensions at all levels: in the community of nations, in the marriage of economy and society within a nation, between husband and wife, between parents and children within families, and between conflicting tugs within ourselves. Over a century ago, de Tocqueville saw how successful America was in reconciling tensions among growth, cohesion, and order to operate a democracy in an industrial economy. The same tensions, along with the opportunities and the dangers that always accompany them, are here today.

TAKE-AWAYS

In assessing the relevance and value of what they learn, business executives often talk about "take-aways"—that is, what are they going to do differently Monday morning? What can we "take away" from the understanding that knowledge itself will be the key factor in shaping the future of our economy and our lives? How can we put that understanding to productive use?

The take-away for enterprise is to grow and gain competitive advantage by investing in learning and by increasing the knowledge-value of the company's offerings in the marketplace. After two decades of anticipation, the productivity gains from investing in information technology are finally registering. Strategies and investments in technologies that emphasize knowledge are the logical next step. Many will look for an immediate payoff, unwilling to accept the current embryonic quality of knowledge-based products and services. Others will ignore this new field or will wait to see early returns before they pay serious attention. The pace of change, however, is very rapid, and those who are unwilling or unable to adapt and use knowledge-based technologies will find themselves too "late to market" and stuck in mature and declining businesses.

The smart ones, however, will begin now to adopt humanized, knowledge-intensive technologies to redefine their businesses and restructure their organizations to support those technologies. They will start with a vision of the knowledge-based future and will do everything they can to reach it. A decade from now they will no longer be in the same business.

For individuals, the first take-away is a shift in the paradigm and the perspective we have of learning and an expansion to worlds never thought of before. Changing the way we look at the world is a mighty big action. It will inevitably alter the ways we learn and earn. Whether we are preparing for employment or already employed, we must commit to lifelong learning, both supported by a federal focus on building economic strength and nourished by corporate commitment to the constant upgrading of employees. Individual employees must embrace continual work-related studies. People in droves are abandoning schools as the path to a better life. Embracing lifelong work-related learning, however, will return us to this path.

For consumers, the take-away is a panoply of smarter products and services that will improve the quality of our lives and broaden our abilities and horizons. Just as surely, all that smart stuff will also bring new problems to our individual lives and to society. Nevertheless, these products and services are on their way, and the flood is just beginning.

As with the earlier waves of computers, faxes, modems, and cellular phones in the information era—and still earlier waves of cars, electric lights, planes, and television in the industrial era—there will be early enthusiasts and late-arriving phobics. And just as happened with all the earlier advances, the new generation of smart products and services will eventually become integral parts of our everyday lives.

For educators, the take-away is that schools and institutions can rehabilitate themselves, reverse their decline, and enter into an era of rebirth. But first they must redefine students and school-related learning as only a slice of a new educational pie. No longer the totality of education, these institutions must become specialized niche players in a more diversified world of learning. When they adopt this larger perspective and join the renaissance in business-related education, they can become more productive and service oriented. They can build meaningful alliances and encourage competition. They can embrace risk, results, and rewards as essential in school-oriented learning. They can invest in research and technology. They can join the knowledge revolution instead of being swept away by it.

When facing change of major proportions, one must first create an awareness of its magnitude and importance. Therefore, the coming dominance of business in redefining learning deserves the widest possible discussion and debate. Everyone has a role to play in these exchanges: executives, educators, government officials, and the general public. Once people become aware of the opportunities as well as the challenges that lie ahead, education will move to the front burner as one of the most pressing issues in America. Then we can begin to take the steps necessary—in business, education, and government—to ensure our strength as a competitor in a global economy. The national interest has always been a motivator for basic change. In early America the drive was for national unity and later for national defense; today it is for economic health.

At the personal level, work to establish lifelong learning as the norm in your workplace, community, and home. If the half-life of most training and knowledge is but a handful of years, learning must be continuous. Therefore, develop a lifelong learning strategy for yourself. If you are thirty, what will you need to know by the time you are thirty-five or forty? This may be as simple as "conquer computer phobia and become computer literate by taking night school classes in word processing and spreadsheets." Or it may be more comprehensive, such as "take courses to improve my management skills, learn a foreign language, and get approval to take two weeks per year in company-sponsored customer service training."

If you have people who report to you, have them develop their learning strategies, too. What skills are essential to their jobs? Is it English, math, welding, sales training? Identify needs and specify realistic steps to meet them. Create both short-term objectives, midrange goals, and a lifelong learning vision, and revise and update them annually.

Do the same thing with your customers. What will you learn about them in the next twelve months? What can your products and services teach them in the next five years? Spend at least as much time educating customers as employees. In business, these are your two major learning segments—and even as you identify them as distinct groups, be certain to mix them together. Companies with walls between customer and employee are sealing off opportunities for the two groups to learn from each other and incurring unnecessary extra expenses. At least a quarter of the people in employee training sessions should be customers, suppliers, distributors, and the like. Similarly, in customer-focused sessions, a quarter of the participants should be noncustomers.

In your dialogues, don't get sidetracked by the misperception that business will take over schools. Yes, there will be more private management and ownership of schools; but this is a sideshow. What's most important is outside of school systems; it's customers and the workforce. If you are in business, keep the focus on these segments. If you are in education, encourage your schools to benefit from the success that the free market model offers.

It is also essential that you master the distinctions among data, information, and knowledge. If these are still interchangeable buzzwords, then you have yet to discover the power knowledge has to move your company and career forward. As an exercise, figure out how your business is different when it is based on each of the three. First, identify a product or service and its relevant data. Next, ask what it would take to elevate these data to information. Third, determine what it would take to make that item knowledge based. Such a sequence for detergent, for example, might result in a product that was fabric sensitive. For an elevator it might mean the addition of a traffic modulation capability. Whenever this process identifies a knowledge-based characteristic, ask how your company could apply that characteristic to your own products or services. These are not difficult things to do, they are only unfamiliar. Above all, the purpose is to establish a new perspective that, with familiarity, will become a habit of mind.

Another useful step is to reassess where you fit in the new learning value chain. Remember, the three key links are those who create and supply the learning materials, those who distribute them, and those who deliver them to students, employees, or consumers. In the wake of the knowledge revolution and its technology, these links are no longer the discrete segments they used to be. As the learning chain goes electronic, students, for example, increasingly will determine which learning suppliers and distributors they want to deal with and will no longer let school administrators mandate this decision. They will choose their learning materials, whether they are electronic or paper based, and they will choose how the subject is taught. If you are in a school system, you have the most radical opportunity to redefine the supply, distribution, and delivery of education. If you are in the knowledge business, or hope to be, your survival and prosperity will depend on how quickly you can redefine your own position in the learning value chain and respond to its new demands.

Since employee education is the fastest growing of all learning segments, you should carefully examine your investment in this most valuable resource. How much does your company spend on employee education, including indirect costs? Amazingly, most companies have no idea. Do you benchmark training and development activities relative to your chief competitors? Holiday Inn, for example, knows that it outspends Sheraton by a factor of five. Collaborate with suppliers, distributors, and other noncompetitors to share educational development costs.

Next, examine the technologies you and your customers use and humanize them. What needs humanizing the most, your products and services or your organization? In each, narrow your focus to specific products, technologies, and activities, asking questions like "Would speech recognition or video make this easier to use?" and "Would telecommuting and teleconferencing improve productivity and morale?" Reduce brick-and-mortar investment in learning and increase your investment in "just-in-time learning" via multimedia electronic networks.

Finally, a major take-away is a better sense of what will and won't work when restructuring. Forget about creating a learning organization; such a notion is pompous, frivolous, or both and not what the experts intended. Instead put your energies into building your learning business, because only when that is in place will you have a real understanding of what "learning organization" means. There are several business developments that have evolved sufficiently to organize around them. For example, since most of the economy is based on services, industrial forms of organization are yielding to service forms, even in manufacturing. Similarly, productivity, networks, and the need to be fast, flexible, and global have become intrinsic to business and are now becoming more common in business organization. Efforts focused on these aspects of organization will yield much more than premature organizing around knowledge and learning.

The seven ways in which knowledge and learning are permeating our businesses, our schools, and our everyday lives are not predictions for the future. These major changes are already taking place, and we must understand and make use of them to profit from knowledge.

Megan's story, which opened this book, is repeated millions of times each day by all ages and levels of society. The skills and technology she used to tell her story will soon become as commonplace as talking on the telephone. Those who cannot or will not see this unfolding historical process will be its victims. They will continue to be plagued by monsters both real and imagined. What or who is the monster threatening our learning throughout our lives? Is it the school system that remains rooted in another age? Is it old declining businesses still operating by rules from an outmoded economic era? Is it the fraying safety net of the welfare state? Is it our society, with its inequalities and violence, which seems so out of place in a knowledge era? Most of these monsters, however real, are relics of the bygone industrial age.

It is also true that we may inadvertently and recklessly create new monsters in a rush to profit from knowledge. While Megan used new technologies to get rid of the monster under her bed without giving it a second thought, many see knowledge-based technology itself as the monster, an unfriendly intruder into our businesses and our lives. Others may think that applying any business practices to schools is monstrous. But if the new learning tools are applied judiciously, we may be able to revive ailing businesses and create exciting new enterprises. We have the tools to expand the horizons of consumers, employees, and students, improving opportunities for employment and raising standards of living. We have the know-how to increase productivity and sharpen our competitive edge in the global economy. We have the means to tame the old monsters and prevent the emergence of new ones. Any technology or institution, old or new, carries with it the potential for good and bad. With this awareness, the choices, as always, are up to us.

THE SEVEN WAYS

First, business is coming to bear the major responsibility for the kind of education that is necessary for any country to remain competitive in the new economy.

Second, the marketplace for learning is being redefined dramatically from K–12 to K–80, or lifelong learning, whose major segments are customers, employees, and students, in that order.

Third, any business can become a knowledge business by putting data and information to productive use, creating knowledge-based products and services that make its customers smarter.

Fourth, a new generation of smart and humanized technologies will revolutionize learning by employees and customers in business before it affects students and teachers in schools.

Fifth, business-driven learning will be organized according to the values of today's information age: service, productivity, customization, networking, and the need to be fast, flexible, and global.

Sixth, schools will embrace businesslike practices to improve their own performance. The three R's will be complemented by the new six R's: risks, results, rewards, relationships, research, and rivalry.

Seventh, the revolution in the way we learn will worsen the already grave division between social classes, requiring us to redress human and social inequities.

NOTES

Chapter 1 **The Reluctant Heir**

1. We wish to acknowledge Lawrence A. Cremin's brilliant history of American education, *American Education: The Colonial Experience 1607–1783* (New York: Harper & Row, 1970), the best source for anyone wanting to pursue this subject in depth. Many of our insights in this section derive from his work.
2. National Commission on Excellence in Education, *A Nation at Risk* (Washington, D.C.: GPO, 1983), 5.
3. 1992 Edition, *Electronic Market Data Book* (Washington, D.C.: Electronic Industries Association, 1992), 24.
4. Peter Drucker, *Post-Capitalist Society* (New York: HarperCollins, 1993), 200.

Chapter 2 **Four Steps to Wisdom**

1. Technically speaking a Thermos bottle doesn't "know." Instead, it isolates what's inside from what's outside by blocking the three different ways heat/cold can move—by conduction (with glass liners), convection (with a near-vacuum space) and radiation (with silvering).

Chapter 3 **The Chatter, the String, and the Can**

1. We wish to acknowledge Alan Kay, who was most helpful to our understanding of the importance of agents.
2. Eric Vogt, MicroMentor, Inc., as reported in "Communiqué," Ernst & Young International Newsletter (Cleveland: April 1993).
3. "Extract, Educational Technology Trends, Public Schools, 1992–93, Sixth Annual Technology Survey of Selected U.S. School Districts," Quality Education Data, Inc. (Denver, Colo.: August 1992); and "Extract, Technology in Public Schools, Selected Data from QED's 12th Annual Installed Base Report on Technology in U.S. Schools" (January 1993).
4. "The Shame of America's Schools," *Macworld* (September 1992).

Chapter 4 **L'earning Power**

1. "An introduction to *Training*'s Annual Analysis of Employer-Provided Training in U.S. Organizations," *Training* (October 1992), 25–55.
2. As reported in *Work-Based Learning: Training America's Workers* (Washington, D.C.: GPO, U.S. Dept. of Labor, Bureau of Apprenticeship and Training, Employment and Training Administration, 1989), *i*.
3. National Center for Manufacturing Sciences, *Insights* (August 1992).
4. Bill Wilson, "Federal Express Delivers Pay for Knowledge," *Training* (June 1991).
5. See, for example, Martha E. Mangelsdorf, "Ground Zero Training: Who Says Small Companies Don't Train Employees?" *Inc.* (February 1993), and Ronald Henkoff, "Companies That Train Best," *Fortune* (March 22, 1993), 62–75.
6. *Harvard Business Review* (January–February 1991), 102.
7. Office of Technology Assessment, "Worker Training: Competing in the New International Economy" (Washington, D.C.: GPO, September 1990), 15.
8. See Jack E. Bowsher, *Educating America* (New York: John Wiley & Sons, Inc., 1989); Nell P. Eurich, *The Learning Industry* (Princeton, N.J.: The Carnegie Foundation for the Advancement of Teaching, 1990); and Lewis J. Perelman, *School's Out* (New York: William Morrow & Co., Inc., 1992).
9. Tom Peters, "Survival Strategies," *Newsletter* (February 10, 1992).

Chapter 5 **The *Last* Thing You Want Is a Learning Organization**

1. Peter Senge argues forcefully for a learning organization in *The Fifth Discipline: The Art & Practice of the Learning Organization* (New York: Doubleday, 1990).
2. Stephen Roach, "Services Under Siege: The Restructuring Imperative," *Harvard Business Review* (September–October 1991).
3. Michael Hammer and James Champy, *Reengineering the Corporation* (New York: Harper Business, 1993).
4. See C. K. Prahalad and Gary Hamel, "The Core Competence of the Corporation, *Harvard Business Review* (May–June 1990), and

James Brian Quinn, *Intelligent Enterprise* (New York: Free Press, 1992).
5. See Alvin Toffler, *Powershift* (New York: Bantam Books, 1990).
6. "Freedom of Ignorance," Bob Pool, *Los Angeles Times* (September 18, 1987), citing tests done by Cal State/Fullerton professor William Puzo for the Center for Civic Education. Other surveys by National Geographic Society and CBS report similar findings.

Chapter 6 **The Six R's**

1. See Philip Glouchevitch, *Juggernaut* (New York: Simon & Schuster, 1992), 130.
2. Ibid., 133.
3. *Fortune* (May 31, 1993) and *BusinessWeek* (April 26, 1993).
4. According to the National Alliance of Business 1990 study, reported in *CIO* magazine (December, 1990). Updated estimates as of 1993 are as high as 200,000 company-school partnerships.
5. *Research and Education Reform: Roles for the Office of Educational Research and Improvement,* (Washington, D.C.: National Academy Press, 1992), 19.
6. See "A New Learning Agenda, 'Putting People First,' " *Institute for Research on Learning* (1993).

ACKNOWLEDGMENTS

Coauthoring this book was a learning process for us both. Working closely together—in Boston or Santa Fe, with occasional stops in Washington and New York—was an experience of collaboration in the truest sense of the word.

Our literary agent, Rafe Sagalyn, deftly guided us in shaping the book from its conception, through chapter outlines, to its completion, giving valuable criticism and advice along the way. At Simon & Schuster, our editor, Fred Hills, skillfully guided us through the hoops and over the hurdles of shaping and publishing a book; Burton Beals provided tough and thorough editing line by line; and Laureen Connelly was always helpful.

Early in the life of the project, Digital Equipment provided some research support. Betsey Cane conducted research on many points and awed us with her ability to tap innumerable databases with skill and good cheer, and Kim Francis was also most helpful. Kathy Tiano and Richard Katz, in Digital's Education Consulting practice, have been enthusiastic and thoughtful commentators throughout the project.

Grateful thanks to Hilary Rochelle, who helped with constant rereadings of the manuscript and with valuable marketing advice. Gerhard Friedrich, who believed in this topic from the beginning, also provided encouragement, leads and advice. Our good friend Eric Vogt, President of MicroMentor and Chairman of InterClass, asked many provocative questions that stimulated our thinking.

We would like to give special thanks to the executives of InterClass (International Corporate Learning Association) whose information and feedback provided great practical and moral support. They include Jeri Thornsberry and Tom Trezise (AT&T), John Greco and Ramesh Ratan (AT&T Bell Labs), Jim Chrz and Nancy Tuyn (Chevrolet), Hubert Saint-Onge (Canadian Imperial Bank of Commerce), John Zitelli (Computer Science Corporation), Don Dinsel (DuPont), Mary Ann Donahue and Kate O'Keefe (Honeywell), Peter Henschel and Susan Stucky (Institute for Research on Learning), Joseph Weber (InterClass), Jeff Farr (KPMG Peat Marwick), Rebecca Philips (Los Alamos National Laboratory), Wayne Townsend (Saturn), Clifford Gilpin (World Bank), and Meg Graham (Xerox).

We visited company executives and school educators in this country and abroad, and we are grateful to everyone who provided insights and ideas. We would also like to thank the many people who provided useful suggestions and read early drafts. These include: Bud Baskin (Arthur Andersen), David A. Bennett (Education Alternatives, Inc.), John Seely Brown (Xerox PARC), Joe Brouilette, Bob Burnside (Center for Creative Leadership), Steve Karol (HMK), Jewell DeWeese and Mike Leven (Holiday Inn), Dee Dickinson (New Horizons for Learning), Ricardo Diez Hochleitner (Club of Rome), D. D. Downs (Downs National Media Literacy), Amy Edmondson (Harvard University), Nell Eurich (Academy for Education Development), Joel Friedman, Larry Greiner (U.S.C.), Larry Howell (Campus America), Keith Martino (Federal Express), Blythe McGarvie (Sara Lee), Jean McGrew (District Superintendent, Glennbrook, Illinois, High Schools), Chris Meyer (Mercer Management), Charlotte Pollard (PO.LAR Associates), Juan Rada, Patricia Reinstein, Richard R. Rowe, Howard M. Schwartz (Gemini Consulting), Peter Senge (MIT), William Ury (Harvard Negotiation Project), Margot Brill-Wygant (College of Santa Fe).

Mimi Chase-Trujillo ably cared for administration of the project and book marketing, and we value her friendship.

We are grateful to Stan's wife, Bobbi Davis, for the many lunches and book titles she created during her own busy workday, until the monster was tamed.

STAN DAVIS
Chestnut Hill, Boston,
Massachusetts, U.S.A.

JIM BOTKIN
Santa Fe,
New Mexico, U.S.A.

INDEX

About the Authors

STAN DAVIS is a distinguished public speaker, author, and business adviser, most known for his creative thinking and mind-stretching perspectives. His *2020 Vision* was named *Fortune* magazine's Best Management Book of 1991 ("the most mind-bending of the bunch") and his influential work *Future Perfect* received Tom Peters' "Book of the Decade" Award in 1989. This is what led Federal Express, in 1993, to grant him their first "Visionary of the Year Award." His eight books appear in fifteen languages and he addresses audiences throughout the world. Dr. Davis consults about the strategy, technology, management, and organization of both major corporations and fast-growing enterprises. He taught for two decades at the Harvard Business School, and Columbia and Boston universities. He lives and works in Chestnut Hill, Boston, Massachusetts.

JIM BOTKIN is cofounder and president of InterClass—the International Corporate Learning Association, a consortium of *Fortune* 500 companies focused on new learning opportunities. An expert in the theory and practice of organizational learning and an internationally known speaker and writer on the future of business and education, he has addressed hundreds of business and public audiences worldwide. He wrote the award-winning Club of Rome report *No Limits to Learning,* which has been translated into more than a dozen languages. A former Director of the Salzburg Seminar, he is an "Honorary Citizen" of Salzburg, Austria. He has an MBA and Doctorate from the Harvard Business School and was on the faculty of the Harvard Graduate School of Education. He is a Fellow at the University of Texas at Austin and a member of The Club of Rome. He lives and works in Santa Fe, New Mexico.